The Professor & The Public

Leo M. Franklin 1870–1948

The & Professor The Public

The Role of the Scholar in the Modern World

The Franklin Memorial Lectures

Volume XX

compiled by Goldwin Smith

*Holder of the Leo M. Franklin Memorial Lectureship
in Human Relations
Wayne State University for the year 1970–1971*

WAYNE STATE UNIVERSITY PRESS, DETROIT   1972

Published simultaneously in Canada
by the Copp Clark Publishing Company
517 Wellington Street, West
Toronto 2B, Canada.

Library of Congress Cataloging in Publication Data

Smith, Goldwin Albert.
    The professor & the public.

    (Leo M. Franklin lectures in human relations, v. 20)
    CONTENTS: Smith, G. The gates of excellence.—Rowse,
A. L. The scholar & responsibility to the public.—Hexter, J. H.
The historian & his society.
    1. Learning and scholarship—Addresses, essays, lectures.
2. History—Philosophy. I. Rowse, Alfred Leslie, 1903–   II.
Hexter, Jack H., 1910–   III. Title. IV. Series.
AZ361.S553   301.44'5   72–2088
ISBN 0–8143–1477–5

    Grateful acknowledgment is made to Temple Beth El for
financial assistance in publishing this volume to commemorate
Rabbi Leo M. Franklin, the spiritual leader of Temple Beth El
from 1899 to 1941 and Rabbi Emeritus thereafter till his death
in 1948.

The Leo M. Franklin Lectures and the Holders of the Leo M. Franklin Memorial Lectureship in Human Relations at Wayne State University

†Vol. I   (1951)   **Toward Better Human Relations**
Lloyd Allen Cook, *Professor of Educational Sociology*

Vol. II*   (1952)   **Our Troubles with Defiant Youth**
Fritz Redl, *Professor of Social Work*

†Vol. III   (1953)   **American Foreign Policy and American Democracy**
Alfred H. Kelly, *Professor of History*

†Vol. IV   (1954)   **Contemporary Problems in Religion**
Harold A. Basilius, *Professor of German*

†Vol. V   (1955)   **Problems of Power in American Democracy**
Arthur Kornhauser, *Professor of Psychology*

†Vol. VI   (1956)   **The City in Mid-Century**
H. Warren Dunham, *Professor of Sociology*

Vol. VII   (1957)   **The Nature of Being Human**
Marie I. Rasey, *Professor of Educational Psychology*

† *Out of print.*   * *Unpublished.*
Titles of volumes differ in some instances from titles of lectures as originally announced.

7

9

Contents

1
The Gates of Excellence

By Goldwin Smith
Professor of History, Wayne State University

*P*aul Tillich wrote wisely about the fact that a sense of power and a sense of insecurity lie uneasily together in the soul of modern man. Despite the achievements and the emerging promises of science and technology somehow there has been a lack of integration in most individuals and in all societies. More and more the lord of nature, man is not yet the master of himself. The dreams that shine at one hour are often dimmed the next. More power moves side by side with more doubt and more fear.

Dangerous and baffling questions refuse to get out of the way of marching man. What can be done about the problems of booms and depressions; ideologies that run wild; foreign plots and counterplots; incredible muddle on every hand; the organization of trade and commerce—the complex riddles of economic cooperation, competition, and conflict; the tangled arguments about production and distribution among the tariff-ridden national states of the world; the increase of the world's population? Our planet is filled with constant shadows and dangers of war, the voices of the homeless and the hungry, the problems of soil erosion and exhaustion, the pollution of the land, the sky, and the water.

Many voices try to convince men that there will be no difficulty in reaching the fat lands of the future and the smooth highways of plenty and peace. Truth, it is said, can still be purchased at the booths in Vanity Fair. Meanwhile more than half the population of our planet can neither read nor write. Two thirds of the people in the world have a life expectancy of less than thirty-five years at birth. Sixty-five percent of the world's population has only twenty percent of the world's income.

Questions multiply. Is the trampling power of the new science bringing a disintegration of the individual personality? Are there too many captive minds and too many crowd compulsions? Do the depersonalized and pitiless gods of the machine take too much tribute? Does the tide of moral lethargy, agnosticism, atheism, mechanized illusions, and ethical neutrality threaten to overwhelm and push into oblivion the religious, national, and ethical imperatives, the funded experience that have ruled and guided men for centuries? How did men ever come to believe that scientific knowledge would enable them to wipe away every social and personal evil in the world? Did they forget the words of Job? "Yet man is born unto trouble, as the sparks fly upward."

Is modern man being prodded and lashed along in his search for power by nameless hungers and a nagging spiritual loneliness that he cannot explain or understand? Has he tossed away so much of his cultural heritage that he fears in the secret chambers of his being that the shining promises of material and secular progress, of triumphant nationalism and an earthly paradise will turn to ashes in his hands? Where are the seed-plots of tomorrow's history? How many of yesterday's truths and traditions have been tossed away, defeated, or destroyed? Will new tribes of barbarians, so clever and shrewd and strong, stride out to conquer and control? "History," says C. P. Snow, "is merciless to failure."

What must a man do? What must he believe? asks Browning's Rabbi Ben Ezra:

> Now, who shall arbitrate?
> Ten men love what I hate
> Shun what I follow, slight what I receive.
> Ten, who in ears and eyes
> Match me; we all surmise
> They this thing, and I that; whom shall
> my soul believe?

This age of ours has dug a deeper gulf between itself and its past than any generation in history. "We have broken up the roads behind us," says Geoffrey Bruun, "and we are secretly dismayed by our desolate and incommunicable singularity."

Today, many young men and women are sincerely convinced that the errors of an older generation produced a society bedevilled by rivalries and pressures, hypocrisy, exploitation, boredom, discontent, and frustration. They see themselves as prophets of a new world striving to be born. They send out storm warnings. They condemn some of their fellow students who seem to be conditioned and conforming. They insist that there is no place, in a dynamic and changing world, for values and attitudes that their parents held to be true and good. With the self-assurance that belongs to youth, these young people declare that they want to destroy what they feel is a corrupt society and set up their own counter-culture. With what Lionel Trilling has called their "radical subjectivity" they repudiate the goals and gods of their fathers and mothers. They insist, as the young have often done, upon the importance of feeling, of private experience, of self-discovery. They talk much of freedom but sometimes seem to be afraid of life.

A few of these young people live in a world of tension and hernia, "tossed to and fro and carried by every wind of doctrine." They often delight in exhibitionism and destruction as they burn books and blow up laboratories—symbols of a way of life they condemn. They have often moved towards intellectual nihilism, denying the relevance of reason, logic, and history. George Santayana once defined a fanatic as a man who redoubled his energy as he lost sight of his goal.

These young people forget—or never knew—that historians always have the last word—or at least the last word but one. They forget—or never knew—Edmund Burke's insistence upon the value of continuity in human affairs "without which men would become as flies in summer." They forget—or never knew—the words of Richard Hooker: "Zeal needeth both ways a safe guide." Nor do they know that in the past many sincere and impatient innovators, men who were determined to destroy tradition and start all over again, failed to build anything that did not topple soon.

Some perplexed parents have tried to listen, understand, and encourage their young. Others have reacted with impatience to what they consider the wrong-headed aspirations of youth who do not know how to cope with the world and its harsh realities. Still others have traveled their accustomed roads, certain that the protesting youths will soon become middle-aged, scarred and armed by experience.

"Your young men shall see visions and your old men shall dream dreams." The fathers insist that their sons will never reach the marble palaces of their cities of desire. The fathers often say that their sons, too, will wander and stray abroad and make mistakes. No matter how many reforms are achieved there will never be paradise this side of Jordan. *L'ineptie consiste á vouloir conclure.* The names of many radical groups have only resonance, except to the chosen. At last Miuskin learns that "paradise is a difficult matter, Prince, much more difficult than it seems to your good heart." Two centuries ago David Hume concluded that all belief is more properly an act of the affective than of the cogitative part of man's nature. "Disputes are multiplied," he wrote, "as if everything were uncertain and these disputes are managed with the greatest warmth, as if everything were certain."

Restless and sincere young men and women are not easily satisfied by answers that they consider dusty and evasive, sometimes untrue. They want to set right the things that they find wrong in this world. They are certainly mistaken about some things. They may be very right about others. Because they are human beings they sometimes change their minds. In the New York *Times* of May 9, 1971, were these words of a young man from Buffalo, New York: "I guess last year we really believed the apocalypse was the day after tomorrow. When it didn't come, we sort of retreated to the day before yesterday. Now, we know that things are bleak but we know that we have 30 or 40 years ahead of us and we have to deal with that."

Democracy cannot do without argument, without the "liberty to know, to utter and to argue freely, according to conscience." Without thought and action there is no advance. The status quo has many vanishing assets. Long ago Michael Faraday remarked that "in knowledge that man is only to be condemned and despised who is not in a state of transition." There is no substitute for careful thought and watchful scrutiny.

Many an abuse has lingered because nobody has taken the time to look to see if anything was wrong.

> "He has nothing on," said the little child.
> "Oh, listen to the innocent," said the father.
> And one whispered to the other what the child had said: "He has nothing on!"
> The Emperor writhed because he knew it was true. But he thought that the procession must go on now, so he held himself stiffer than ever and the Chamberlain held up the invisible train.

Do we say nothing when we see the Emperor without clothes? If the people in the crowd around us speak about the beauty of the Emperor's purple and ermine robe, what must we do? Do we stay silent and yield to the mass mind and spirit? The smothering concepts of conformity may be dangerous and evil. All men cannot be compelled to think the same thing and it would not be a good thing if they did. Today we hear many voices, insistent and hypnotic, proclaiming the importance of conformity. That passion for conformity has often been confused with the ideas and ideals of democracy and this is perilous nonsense. With robot conformity can come the death of the spirit and the paralysis of the mind. "If I were an ant I should play the part of an ant; in fact I am not an ant, and if try to play the part of an ant I shall end in the care of a psychiatrist."

We must not forget that as a state and a people we must fear and defend ourselves against the passionate and vehement voices and pens that insist upon patterns of conformity. The "mass mind" can be a deadly enemy to a democratic state. If we do not take thought, if we are apathetic, then we have in fact decided to face quietly "the slow white death that waits for privilege in defeat." It is one of our tasks to stop the trampling march of those who want to destroy what they cannot understand.

It is true that we must always be ready to change our minds. Those of us who have crossed the great divide of thirty must not take pride in some of our forts too long. They may have become indefensible. When I was a young instructor in history I described in one of my more brilliant lectures the "impregnable fortress of Singapore." I was mistaken. So, too, were the experts in the British War Office upon whose judgment I relied. Let us beware of what John Stuart Mill once called "the deep slumber of a decided opinion."

We must be prepared, as I remarked a moment ago, to change our minds. Nearly two centuries ago, with precision and grace, Benjamin Franklin penned these words:

> Mr. President, I confess that there are several parts of this Constitution that I cannot at present approve, but I am not sure that I shall never approve them. For having lived long, I have experienced many instances of having been obliged by better information or fuller consideration to change opinions even on important subjects, which I once thought right but found to be otherwise.

Many of the impatient young people who object to what is often called the Establishment are students in our colleges and universities today. It is the task of the professors to assist these students in their search for knowledge and understanding. The first duty of a university is not to develop skills but to develop a breadth of view, a sense of proportion and perspective, a sound judgment, and a depth of mind. This is the meaning and goal of liberal education. This is its task. In our honest regard for things that are "socially useful" it is wise to remember that the training of the mind and spirit of a human being is still a desirable thing, justified in itself, regardless of any social consequences. Said Aristotle: "As the state was created to make life possible, so it exists to make it good."

A few years ago, Professor Clinton Rossiter of Cornell University wrote this: "We stand at one of those rare moments in history when a nation must choose between greatness and mediocrity." H. G. Wells once remarked that we are in a race between education and catastrophe. Some men may consider these statements too extreme, the prospects too fearful. Some professors and teachers, satisfied with their role in society and their success in teaching and research, may, like Bunyon's Sloth and Simple, be convinced that we are safe, quite safe.

> *Watchful the Porter:* But how does it happen that you come so late? The sun has set.
> *Christian:* I had been here sooner but that, wretched man that I am, I slept in the arbor that stands on the hill-side. . . .
> *Simple* said: I see no danger.
> *Sloth* said: Yet a little more sleep.
> And *Presumption* said: Every tub must stand upon its own bottom.
> And so they lay down to sleep again.

Let us not be deceived, careless, or apathetic. Jean Paul said: "If you do not use your eyes for seeing, you will use them for weeping." There is no doubt of the kind of planet we inhabit. Our world is in grave disarray. Three hundred years ago John Milton said that he would not praise "a fugitive and cloistered virtue, unexercised and unbreathed, that never sallies forth to seek her adversary." We do not have to sally forth to find those who declare that they would, if given the chance, destroy the heritage of Western civilization. Those who talk and write nonsense and choose to fly in the infinite inane should be challenged and answered always. If we pay no attention, if we are meek, if we are reluctant to reply and resist, if we are not prepared to watch the ramparts then we may clatter down to destruction. "It never troubles the wolf how many sheep there be."

At the battle of Isandhlwana fought in 1879 a British regiment was totally destroyed, mostly because there were no screwdrivers to open the ammunition boxes. Professors and generals must have available supplies. Their campaigns must be carefully planned. They must have reserves and they must not wobble or break ranks. They must not sit in isolated and insulated places, fingering the crumpled edges of their notes, lifting their eyes above the students, above the public, taking themselves more seriously than their work, sometimes preferring peace to combat for the truth. These calm habit routines can be dangerous. Professors—and other men too—must remember that the Buddha put down ritualism as one of the Ten

Fetters that bind men to illusion and prevent them from being enlightened.

Do we professors write and talk, now and then, too much about formulas and categories and not enough about vital forces within men hammered out by the rivers and dreamed of on the lonely frontiers of the mind? Do we sometimes live and write and talk too much to ourselves, we happy few? Are we often almost out of touch with the new era we are helping to shape?

Some men are not out of touch. They see the tragedy, comedy, melodrama, farce, and casual superficiality of many aspects of our world. They see some of the pitfalls ahead. They do not sit back and wait to see what will happen.

These men are the great teachers, the real leaders in the colleges and universities of our country. They are the committed and passionate and vivid men who stir the spirits and trigger the adrenal glands of their students. In the reign of Elizabeth I, Sir Philip Sidney wrote, "To what purpose should our thoughts be directed to various kinds of knowledge, unless room be afforded for putting it into practice so that public advantage may be the result?"

We have all known some great teachers whom we will not forget, civilized and sensitive men, conscious always of the living past, filled with an abiding wonder and curiosity about the mysterious and magnificent universe. In this university, for instance, no student who left a classroom where Professor William Bossenbrook lectured was ever the same again. When Professor Bossenbrook talked about the trade routes to the East you could almost see the sails of the great spice ships and hear the camels grunt by the walls of Trebizond. You saw, or almost saw, the ceiling of the Sistine Chapel being painted and felt the agony and genius of the creator. You almost saw Thomas Becket murdered in the gloom of a vast cathedral. Some pedants pointed out that Professor Bossenbrook made errors in names and dates. Turenne once said: "He who has made but few mistakes has made but little war."

The proper business of professors lies in great waters. They must not linger like lotus eaters within the narrow seas, wearing out their lives in impotence and stultification. Men who teach in the classrooms, who speak in their communities, men who write books and articles, sometimes do not seem to realize how much they may be doing to put a stamp upon their times.

In these days of tumbling events and a babel of voices in the streets and committee rooms of our land, we see a slow erosion of excellence on almost every hand. It is a time to remember that if our sons and daughters are not well taught and trained then the whole basis of our survival is in jeopardy.

The word *paideia* in Greek means education. It also means civilization and culture. The Greeks believed that all their achievements rested upon education, the love for and the pursuit of knowledge, the improvement of all the high powers of the human mind. Men, they said, must learn to think. Many years later, Pascal wrote these words: "Thought maketh the whole dignity of man. Therefore endeavor to think well, for thought is the only true morality."

The modern professor, as all the generations of teachers before him, must endeavor to think well. He betrays his kind and his calling if he goes screaming into the street with blood in his eyes and a gun in his hand. The professor is a valuable citizen of the state. He should also be the keeper of common sense, the guardian of knowledge, the doctor of the soul. If he is one of the true professors then the students should come to his side and his feet. They should remember that "the best way towards greatness is to mix with the great."

In the great universities of the United States there are thousands of students. Only a few will become professors. The rest will not lecture. They will not write. Most of them will become doctors, lawyers, politicians, business men, bankers, missionaries, priests and preachers, teachers in our schools. They are, most of them, going into the big outside to do practical things.

When a professor looks out at the rows of students in his classroom he swiftly sees that some of them are lukewarm and apathetic. Not all are filled with an indefeasible desire to know. Some refuse to listen or even to read the textbook, their main stockade against the terrors of the unknown. They do not realize that the road to knowledge is often hazardous and hard. "Learn not," says the proverb, "and know not." And we all recall Oliver Goldsmith's line about the "loud laugh that spoke the vacant mind."

In almost every classroom there are the eager and able students. Now and then there come into our courses and seminars the outstanding, the really exceptional students, the unusual people who may appear at any time in any place. What stimulus, what recognition will they find in our vast and impersonal modern university? Independent thought can be easily frustrated, little sparks and flames snuffed out. The unusually gifted young people must plow lonely furrows at best. To whom shall they turn in that first moment "when a great thought strikes along the brain and flushes all the cheek?" How many professors can take the time these days—even if they have the understanding—to cope with the growing pains of excellence? How shall we discern, select, and train the heralds for the future who must be our guards and guides in the world of tomorrow, these young people who might provide us, before it is too late, with some of the answers that we have not yet found? Schools and universities do not exist solely to train the superior students. Nor do they exist to neglect or bore the gifted.

My conviction grows daily stronger that we must find and educate as many young people with ability and promise as we can. True, we have many scholarships and fellowships. But we do not have enough. There is no excuse for wasting any of our natural resources, including brains.

There are other problems of importance to us all. It is sometimes difficult, for instance, to convince an undergraduate student that if he is to become an educated man he must know something about the past, about Archimedes and Plato, about St. Thomas Aquinas, about Magna Carta, about the Spanish Armada and the New Deal, perhaps even about the ancient gods and the rifled tombs of predynastic Egypt and of Ur, or neolithic man, that half-conjectured, enigmatic shape, standing at the portals of the timeless deep. The undergraduate may say and feel with emphasis that such things are now not relevant to what he calls the "modern age." All of us who face students in the class-room know that they are much interested in the present, the here and now, the contemporary world in all its concreteness and complexity. From childhood they have been bombarded with assertions that the new is to be preferred to the old, that they should savor in a hurry, that the lessons of the past are only tenuously related to modern problems. Can they be shown that "the roots of the present lie deep in the past"?

It is true that many students and professors interested in the fields of modern science and mathematics cannot communicate well with professors of English who cannot describe the Second Law of Thermodynamics. In *The Two Cultures and the Scientific Revolution,* C. P. Snow remarked that "the great edifice of modern physics goes up, and the majority of the cleverest people in the Western world have about as much insight into it as their neolithic ancestors would have had." It is not easy for a professor of English or of history to talk (with a sure hope of being understood) to a professor or student of physics who moves as a stranger in the world of literature and history. C. P. Snow is quite right in pointing to the great gap that exists today between the men of science and the rest of us, and the failure of communication between these two groups, these two cultures.

Of course, we are well aware that there are far

more obstacles to effective communication than those
that exist between the scientists and the experts in the
fields of the humanities and the social sciences. Most
of us here this evening—professors, doctors, lawyers,
students, members of many professions—have attended
conferences about such problems as research and
teaching, the communication gaps in our society, the
dichotomy between words and action in the world of
politics. We have all noted that some planners of conferences had too much space and did not know how to
fill it. We have listened, sometimes with glazed eyes
and mounting irritation, to sincere and earnest speakers talking about the importance of trail-blazing, the
power of the people, the oppression of American youth
and the answers to questions that almost nobody ever
asked. Sometimes we have listened to the homoge-
nized propaganda of Madison Avenue, were subjected
to barrages of nonsense from speakers with whom we
disagreed, were at least slightly alarmed by the rhe-
toric of those who saw the headlong deliquescence of
American civilization. Later we smiled and drank
coffee together. Discussion was often a series of statements passing into oblivion. Frequently, there was no
real communication despite the repeated statements
that the conference had been, in the language of the
cliché expert, "a rich and meaningful experience."

I turn now to a related theme. It is often difficult

to explain to our students, whether they are working in the world of science or elsewhere, how great are the pleasures of some professors who study old manuscripts, the books written by men who were once held as gods for their wisdom; who prowl and dig in the villages and caves of Kenya and Peru searching for the teeth and bones of our remote ancestors; who peer through telescopes towards the edge of space; who explore the subatomic universe; who work with engineers and preachers and priests and rabbis; who help make laws and governments; who join with artists in making things of beauty; who weep and praise and kneel. All these things the students may not understand. There are numerous problems of communication. Have most of us really begun to comprehend that there are in fact many cultures and subcultures in the Western world and that there are now few things more necessary to comprehend?

There are other problems. Those of us who read journals and newspapers and peer at the shelves of bookstores know that thousands of new books roll from the presses every year. Some of them are not good books. They should be marked "Dead on Arrival." These are the books that many of our students read, particularly if the title and content seem relevant to the present age.

If a student does not read a good book then he

will read something else, a substitute, something that is second best. If we are content to allow, or by our silence encourage, the students to read the second best and the third best, then that which is the very best can easily slip into oblivion. If we are too patient or careless then we may find ourselves faced with an ever-increasing flood of the tinsel, the shoddy, the cheap. It is easy for students—and sometimes professors too—to plunge into the thick of thin things and squander and steal time. Distressing and ill-considered assertions will continue to be made by individuals who are willing to blur and distort the already complicated truth by oversimplified statements and cheap formulas. Enemies of our civilization can come armed with cheap books as well as good guns. If they have their way, then the best will yield to the good, the good to the mediocre, the mediocre to dust and moths and rust.

Will we quietly file away the hinges of our avowed principles? How far shall we soothe the un-eliminated ape at the expense of the undeveloped angel? Will our culture soon slither into mediocrity and reach the level of some of the voices that bawl into the contaminated ether today? How low is the lowest common denominator? "And what is Caliban to do, except live lonely and dig a deep hole?"

"An excellent plumber," wrote John W. Gardner, "is infinitely more admirable than an incompetent philosopher. The society which scorns excellence in plumbing because plumbing is a humble activity and tolerates shoddiness in philosophy because it is an exalted activity will have neither good plumbing nor good philosophy. Neither its pipes nor its philosophy will hold water."

A professor cannot fulfill his function in society if he does not try to communicate his knowledge to other men. If he fails to do this then his research, to use Bolingbroke's words, is "at best but a specious and ingenious form of idleness." All of us who write books and articles should remember that we are not adding much to the knowledge of men if what we write slips into oblivion as soon as our fellow scholars read it. In the Preface to *Don Quixote*, Cervantes said that his aim was to write so that "the simple shall not be wearied and the grave shall not despise it."

Not long ago, I recall reading a few paragraphs by Professor Boyd Shafer, the Executive Secretary of the American Historical Association, in which he said that he hoped that the writers of articles for the *American Historical Review* might try to write with a little more thyroid power, a bit more zoom and zest, more active verbs and fewer ox-cart paragraphs. Many of us have read accurate but boring books written by authors who have never lifted their eyes from the documents, have never wondered if George Washington

liked kidney pie, have forgotten what words the sol-
diers must have used at Gettysburg. "He that will
write well in any tongue," said Roger Ascham in the
sixteenth century, "must follow this counsel of Aristotle, 'to speak as the common people do, to think as
wise men do; and so should every man understand
him, and the judgment of wise men allow him.'"

There are some professors who never use a semi-
colon injudiciously but they cannot write well. I think
sometimes of what a seventeenth-century French
writer remarked when the author of an epic poem
called attention to the fact that he had carefully
obeyed all of the rules of Aristotle: "I am grateful to
him for having obeyed the rules of Aristotle but I am
very angry at Aristotle for having compelled him to
write so dull a poem."

Is it not possible that some professors write too
much pretentious prose, filled with fog-belts, incanta-
tions, and unintelligible arguments? Professor P. W.
Bridgman, Nobel Prize winner in physics in 1946, in-
cluded a sentence in his *Reflections of a Physicist* with
which most of us should agree: "I have a distaste for
grandiloquent words which imply something more
philosophic and esoteric than the simple thing that I
see." Some of the learned books and articles that I
have read and you have read were quite divorced from
reality, padded with frantic superficiality, aimless and
irresponsible, filled with contrived epigrams, flaws and

falseness, and containing ideas neither justified by the problems nor relevant to their solution. "It is not necessary to travel around the world to count the cats in Zanzibar." Polysyllables do not always mean the same thing as profundity. "Men stir up a cloud of dust," said Edith Wharton, "and complain that they cannot see."

It is true, of course, that we should have no truck nor trade with the "any word will do" tribe of writers. They are always the foes of clarity, beauty, logic, and truth. It takes much time and a great deal of work to write well. Carl Becker used to say that if the author did not sweat then the reader had to. No society, no profession, can afford for long to have too many drones.

All professors should encourage their students to develop such literary talents as they may possess. "I would make all boys learn English," wrote Sir Winston Churchill many years ago, "and then I would let the clever ones learn Latin as an honor and Greek as a treat. But the only thing I would whip them for is not knowing English. I would whip them hard for that." Such treatment of our students would probably be considered somewhat drastic today. Nevertheless, they should be carefully and patiently trained to speak and write their language well.

For if the trumpet give an uncertain sound, who shall prepare himself for the battle?

So likewise ye, except ye utter by the tongue words

easy to be understood, how shall it be known what is
spoken? For ye shall speak into the air.

There are, it may be, so many kinds of voices in the
world and none of them is without signification.

Therefore if I know not the meaning of the voice I
shall be unto him that speaketh a barbarian, and he that
speaketh shall be a barbarian unto me.

There are also some professors and teachers—and
other men, too—who delay their decisions too long,
frequently asserting that until all of the evidence is in
they must join the shuffling dance of suspended judgment. They will not, they assert, nail their flags to the
mast too soon. What, then, are their students to do?
How can the people in their community and beyond
look to them for clear decisions and sound judgment?
"What came ye forth to see, a reed shaking in the
wind?"

Several years ago I received an interesting letter
from Bernard DeVoto. Here is a paragraph from it:

Sometime ago I dined with and spent a whole evening
talking to a Department of History. The Chairman, an
authority on American Colonial History, committed
himself to the statement that value judgments were not
only impossible and therefore false when made but
vicious as well. After I spent half an hour pursuing him
from point to point I prepared one and asked him

whether in the largest way and allowing for the widest margin and taking into account the greatest number of considerations it was not on the whole better that the colonies separated then if they had remained a part of the British Empire. He answered that one could not say, for how could one know how it would look a thousand years from now. That seems to me to be a long time to wait for science to work out its certainties and I am content to write impressionistically on a shorter time scale. Nobody will be reading him either in a thousand years and I may say that I find it hard to now.

It is clear that Bernard DeVoto did not agree with the chairman of the history department (whose name I never knew) from another university (whose location I never found out). The grounds for the difference of opinion are complicated. Many of the contemporary disputes among professional historians—and in many other parts of the academic world—are not susceptible to clear-cut resolution. To some men it seems desirable to be what is called "original" and to insist that there is nothing so up-to-date as revolution and a toppling of the old leaders and the familiar gods. Other men are of a different opinion.

Other men are indeed of a different opinion. A professor has been described as a man who thinks otherwise. It is a good description. At the same time, every professor should remember that the controversies within his profession do not diminish his responsibility to students and the public. It continues to be his duty to search for the truth and to come back to tell what he has found and why he thinks it is important. That is the hallmark of a good professor, the good craftsman, the member in good standing of the honorable company of scholars.

The historian probes into the past. He is the high priest of continuity. The physicist probes into space and searches out the laws of mass and energy. From the desks and laboratories of other men come insights and conclusions about penicillin, radar, moon rocks, prothrombin, the double helix, and what Alfred North Whitehead called "the complete abstract generality" of mathematics. There are also the writers, artists, musicians, past and present. We are the transient inheritors of all the achievements of mankind. The riches are ours to keep or destroy. Without vigilance, care, and vision, a people may perish and a civilization move to swift decay.

The professors and the teachers are not alone in their concern about the problems of research, teaching, cooperation, and communication. It is the duty and responsibility of all citizens to do all that they can to guide and train the human beings who are their sons and daughters. We shall all be judged. "Fellow-citizens," said Abraham Lincoln, "we cannot escape history. We will be remembered in spite of ourselves. The fiery trial through which we pass will light us down to honor or dishonor to the latest generation."

Some men have called the twentieth century the age of challenge. Others say that modern man is trapped in the triumphs of his own contriving and that this is the age of fear. Still others claim that is is the era of despair. Not long before his death, H. G. Wells wrote his *Mind at the End of Its Tether,* a book of black pessimism. In its pages Wells, so long a believer and crusader in the cause of secular progress, asserted that for man there was no hope. "A remarkable queerness has come over life," he wrote. "It is as if the law of gravitation no longer functioned in our physical world. Everything is moving with increased velocity in every direction. It is the end." Wells was prepared to ring down the curtain on the great drama of human history. Most men are not.

Nobody can look into the future. Conjecture is unnecessary and unwise. We do know that in the hazards of the present hour the people of all the world must rely on intelligence and faith, be patient, and have courage. "All things excellent," said Baruch Spinoza, "are as difficult as they are rare."

It is not an easy task to strive for "whatsoever

things are true, whatsover things are just, whatsoever things are pure, whatsoever things are lovely, whatsoever things are of good report." Said the Greek poet Hesiod: "Before the gates of excellence the high gods have placed sweat." He also said: "But when the height is won, then there is ease."

2
The Scholar and Responsibility to the Public

BY A. L. ROWSE
Fellow of All Souls College, Oxford

$\mathcal{M}$y title, and indeed the title of this series of Franklin Lectures, indicate a modern approach, a rather recent emphasis: for up till yesterday most people would have conceived the scholar to be, of all people, rather remote from the public and public concerns. You may remember Hilaire Belloc's line—"Remote and ineffectual Don"—which expressed the view of the scholar that used to prevail among the public.

Now all that has changed. Perhaps President Franklin Roosevelt began the process of calling professors into consultation over public affairs with the New Deal Brain Trust and Professor Raymond Moley. Since then Washington and Whitehall have not ceased to reverberate with professors—President Kennedy's mainly from Harvard, Prime Minister Harold Wilson's from Oxford and Cambridge. The experiment continues with President Nixon, not usually considered academic in his outlook—but we may be doing him an injustice.

Anyway, the relation of the academic to society has changed: hence the relevance of these lectures. What is the scholar's responsibility to the public today?

I always think that a useful initial approach is through the literal meaning of words. A scholar meant originally, and still means essentially, a schoolman: a man of the schools and universities. The word "responsible" first came into the language in the Elizabethan age. By the seventeenth century it had come to have the meaning "accountable," liable to be called to account. Already in New England as early as 1650 it had come to have the inflection, answerable to a charge—perhaps that is understandable in that Puritan atmosphere. But the Puritans were victorious twice over in the English-speaking world, once in the seventeenth century, and again in the nineteenth. So that it is not surprising that the Victorian sense of the word we inherited has a moral connotation: responsibility involves an obligation or trust; it also bears the sense of reliability.

Are the professors responsible and reliable? How are we to describe the scholar's responsibility to the public?

Most scholars would probably reply that their prime responsibility is to their subject—without prejudice to the question of wider responsibilities, which we will deal with later. All good scholars, I should say, hold that they have an overriding responsibility to truth in their subject, to the pursuit of truth for its own sake.

All the same, how often this rule is honored more in the breach than the observance! Dishonored, I call it: it never ceases to shock me when a scholar plays fast and loose with the truth, will sacrifice what is true for the sake of sectarian prejudice—as with Belloc or Chesterton (but neither of them was a scholar)—or for political *parti pris;* for the sake of some monstrous sociological construct, as with Oswald Spengler; or simply for the sake of playing to the gallery, which has much increased in our time with the mass media and is particularly encouraged in and displayed by television performers.

We constantly hear complaints coming out of Soviet Russia that distortions of what writers know to be the truth are imposed by the very nature of the régime. They are expected to conform to the changing, temporary, and at different times mutually contradictory, demands of politics. The further burden of their complaint is that the best intellectual work cannot be done in such circumstances, that it demands *freedom of the mind,* at least a freer atmosphere to operate in.

These restraints and distortions are probably at their worst in the social sciences, and especially in regard to history—for the whole point of the study of history is that it should be true. If you want a charming fiction, then write a fictitious story, a novel; if you want to put forward some thesis or other, a philosophical construction is more appropriate. I distrust thesis-history, which is so fashionable at present.

History deals with what actually happened, and there can be no graver disservice to truth than to rewrite history to suit the political needs of the moment. You will know that from the beginning of Stalin's rise to power, Trotsky's part in the Russian Revolution— which was second only to Lenin's—was written down, minimized, and then eliminated altogether. As if it had never been, as if Trotsky never existed! Simultaneously, Stalin's role—modest enough in fact—was written up, until with his personal absolutism you would think that Lenin and Stalin made the Revolution, and then Stalin did all the rest, including winning the war.

Recently, with Khrushchev's exposure of Stalin the line was to write him down—"personality cult," etc. Until, with Khrushchev's own fall, Stalin is now graded somewhat up again.

You could draw a graph in which the writing of Soviet history went up and down, could be correlated with the party-line of the moment. How infantile!—I use the epithet with reason, for such behavior is not consonant with an adult, responsible society.

This kind of distortion, blatant and ludicrous in regard to history, also obtains in literary scholarship, where people are even more liable to be taken in by it, for it is not so flagrantly obvious. This was brought home to my personal attention in the year of Shakespeare's quatercentenary, when I wrote my biography of him. Shakespeare scholars in Soviet Russia were very hard put to it to make him conform to crude and callow Marxist theory, the populist humbug of an—in fact—exceedingly *un*democratic society (in truth, the dictatorship of army and bureaucracy against a people).

Actually Shakespeare was one of the most conservative and conformist of writers, on the side of authority. Living as he did with the recent memory of the ferocities of the Wars of the Roses, and with the catastrophe of the English Civil War not far away, he knew how precarious social order is, how thin the crust of civilization upon which we live—and, when challenged by civil conflict and destroyed, into what dark waters we plunge! Besides, a sensitive, skeptical man, he would never opt for the certain cruelties of revolution for the hope of dubious hypothetical benefits.

Even in the physical sciences we witnessed a similar distortion, with the official promotion of Lysenko's erratic theories on evolutionary genetics.

But Russians, and Germans, are given to overmuch theorizing. English-speaking peoples prefer the factual and the common sense. As the great physiologist, Sir Charles Sherrington, says in *Man on his Nature* —"a fact does not decay"—with the implication that theories do. Nor need we be too skeptical about the process of establishing fact, or even states of mind, the possibility of historical knowledge: which is really another form of *la trahison des clercs*. We have only to look around us to see to what an extent the medieval mind survives—the ubiquitous belief in astrology witnessed by the newspapers; some minds are positively prehistoric; while you can observe a few types about in the streets that have only recently descended from the trees.

As the historian Lecky observed, "Men will believe anything against the evidence, or in spite of the evidence; they will hardly ever believe anything because of the evidence." This is the final reason why we scholars should never deviate from truth: it is our very lifeblood, our *raison d'être*. It is our duty and responsibility, first and last, to keep the wells of truth pure and undefiled.

So much for the distortions that arise from external pressures upon the scholar. What about the distortions arising from within, the question of bias?

Let us be candid about this: it is hardly possible to avoid all bias—one cannot jump out of one's own skin. Or, to discriminate further: one might say that there is a whole spectrum of subjects, of academic disciplines, going from those where the liability to bias is largest to those where it is at its smallest for all practical purposes hardly exists. This range roughly runs from the social sciences or humanities to the physical sciences (themselves not exempt, as we have seen with Lysenko), and so up to the abstract disciplines of mathematics or logical analysis.

In fact, even logic is influenced by personal or social factors, as anyone who observes the history of logic can discern. For example, the correlation of traditional Aristotelian logic with conservatism and Catholicism in the sixteenth century, as against the more modern logic of Ramus which appealed to Protestants.

Even in regard to modern logical analysis, a colleague of mine who set out to study the papers of Frege was shocked to discover that he shared the appalling reactionary nationalism that characterised all too many nineteenth-century German academics. That raises a rather different point, however: a mathematician might hold his political views and his mathematical work in separate compartments. To some extent we can all do that, and scholars do it in greater or lesser degrees: this is rather a subtle matter.

It stands to reason that bias enters in far more largely in the humanities, where personal prejudices are more intimately engaged.

The very word "engaged" reminds us that there is a whole school of thought, led by a leading French writer, Sartre, which inculcates the doctrine that in our intellectual work we *should* be *engagé*. Perhaps it is no wonder he has expressed the view that Soviet Russia exemplifies the ideal of freedom in society. You have to be very clever—or a great ass—to think that. We can have no respect whatever for such thinking: the inversion of sense.

Perhaps historians—along with political theorists, sociologists, and economists—are liable to be most of all affected by bias. What is our responsibility in the matter? What can we do about it?

Well, we can at least be self-aware, candid about our prejudices, declare ourselves at the outset, put our cards on the table.

In this respect eighteenth-century historians—Gibbon and Hume, for example—were more aware of what they were doing than most nineteenth-century historians: it was more in keeping with the cool and skeptical rationalism of the eighteenth century that it should be so. What is so astonishing to me about nineteenth-century people—our grandfathers and great-grandfathers—is the way in which they were hardly aware of their motives, their self-interest and personal inclinations. That helped to give them their extraordinary self-confidence, the power of their certainty and conviction. Of course, they had not had the benefit of reading Freud—it would very much have upset them if they had, might perhaps have knocked them off their perch.

The bias, the prejudice, in the case of an historian

like Carlyle so shrieks at one that one would think it harmless—yet his influence did nothing but harm to a better historian, James Anthony Froude, who had an undertone of skepticism in his nature to which he would have done well to give more expression.

Bias can be more damaging where it is largely unconscious. In his classic *Education of Henry Adams* the author evidently regards himself as the most objective of historians, an impersonal witness of the process. I have a special admiration for Henry Adams, but I am surprised by the extent of his anti-English bias in his large-scale history of the Presidencies of Madison and Monroe. Whatever we may think of the causes of the American Revolution, I cannot but think that, for the outbreak of the war of 1812, honors were at least equally divided (if there were any "honor" in what was virtually a civil war, when Britain was carrying the enormous burden of the struggle against Napoleon's military tyranny over Europe).

Henry Adams' *History* is a very Adamsy book, recognizably carrying on the family views and feuds with the old country. We may conclude that bias is at its most damaging when it is unrecognized, and historians put themselves forward as objective and impersonal. This is what A. J. P. Taylor does with his *Origins of the Second World War,* with its crazy thesis that Hitler was not much more to blame for the Second

World War than we were. It was acclaimed by one of his colleagues as "a flawless masterpiece": it was, of course, flawed from top to bottom. I was shocked by the performance—and not much surprised when four or five nationalist periodicals in Germany took their opportunity to claim—"Germany not responsible for war: Oxford professor says so."

There is no more personal historian writing in Britain than this self-declared exponent of "objectivity" —though, in a journalistic aside, with characteristically irresponsible self-contradiction, he has also declared that there is no such thing as history without bias.

What is the truth of the matter? What is our responsibility? What ought our attitude to be?

First, be self-aware, be conscious of our motives and prejudices, be post-Freudian. Second, be candid, and honest, with ourselves and with the public.

Third, though one cannot jump out of one's skin, one can to a certain extent think oneself out of one's skin. This is the essence of the thinking process—consciously putting what one thinks against the background of what makes one think as one does: putting the one as a numerator over the other as denominator, and so making progress towards some objectivity as the equation works out.

The price of liberty, we are told, is eternal vigilance; it is still more clear that the price of *truth* is eternal vigilance. The achievement of liberty is after all a corporate responsibility, others take part in it; the struggle for truth, to maintain and uphold it, is a more individual and personal matter. In my view it is the lifeblood of civilization—even more than liberty; for it may be achieved in the absence of liberty—as we see with the courageous protests of Pasternak and Solzhenytsin—though this is hampered in its public expression and can hardly be widespread in the absence of liberty.

Perhaps I may call on my own experience as an historian, to illustrate the scholar's problem in the matter of bias and objectivity.

Historians of the sixteenth century—the period of the Renaissance, Reformation and Counter-Reformation (or Catholic Revival)—have nearly all taken sides on these issues: they have been apt to be pro-Reformation or anti-Reformation, simply as they were Protestants or Catholics in their sympathies. This is rather simple-minded—there is nothing more boring than people expounding and defending their *partipris.*

In my own case people are apt to think that on the religious issue of the Elizabethan Age I am simply anti-Puritan. Let me assure you that the case is not so simple as that.

To be candid, I have no *liking* for Puritans—but

that is merely an emotional preference and by no means ends the matter. It is in fact the least important part of it, and is not decisive when it comes to judgment, which should depend upon reason.

Now my ultimate values are not so much ethical as aesthetic: what constitutes ultimate value to me, what redeems life from the mud and gives it quality is the apprehension of the world and experience as beauty. This attitude is not rare among creative writers and artists. It is the position that James Joyce expounded in the long philosophical dialog in his *Portrait of the Artist as a Young Man,* and Robert Bridges told me that he shared this view: it was the message of *The Testament of Beauty.* We may regard it as the religion of Proust, its grandest expression in modern literature is his *A la recherche du temps perdu*—what better epigraph, by the way, for an historian's task?

This attitude is rarer in an historian, certainly to judge from the practice of the common run—perhaps that is why they find it difficult to understand, let alone estimate, an historian who is different.

But there *are* historians who are inspired by or exemplify these values, and they are my mentors. It is hardly surprising that Jacob Burckhardt, the great historian of the Renaissance in Italy, stands at the head of them. There are other things besides his worship of beauty, the respect for the works of men's hands rather than the nonsense they are apt to think, that I share with him. I share his skepticism without illusions about people's pretensions or their callow optimistic expectations. We know how fragile things of beauty are, how liable to destruction by maniac iconoclasts. The twentieth century has corroborated Burckhardt far more than it has liberal optimists or amiable rationalists—like Thomas Jefferson, for example: no century in human history has witnessed a vaster destruction of things of beauty, or for that matter of human lives.

Burckhardt was a pessimist and a skeptic. I am an aggressive skeptic. I specifically isolate one factor in human history as the most destructive and the most cruel—people's faiths and fanaticisms, their certainties (often mutually contradictory) about what is inherently uncertain. In other words, their ideological beliefs and convictions, the nonsenses for which they are ready to kill and have killed in millions all through history—never more so than in this disgraceful century.

Now perhaps you will understand if the saints I venerate are not an odious Luther or Calvin, or a no less odious Loyola—persecutors and inquisitors all—but those men of the middle of the road, moderates and *politiques.* Erasmus and Montaigne, Elizabeth I and William the Silent, Shakespeare, Francis Bacon and Michel de l'Hopital, Grotius and Spinoza—not the extremists on either side who make life intolerable for sensible people in the middle.

That being so, you will perceive that I am not simply anti-Puritan: I detest the fanatics on *both* sides (as again in the twentieth century). However, working as I am in the field of the Elizabethan Renaissance, you will not expect me to approve of people who would proscribe the Shakespearean theatre, prohibit all drama, most music (especially church music), most painting, sculpture and the visual arts—to concentrate on the excruciating delights of perpetual sermonizing and examinations of the conscience.

No: my values are the Renaissance values of Shakespeare, Marlowe, Bacon; Donne, William Byrd, Nicholas Hilliard—not Calvin, Knox, Cartwright, loud-mouthed Perkins or cotton-mouthed Mather.

One might slightly adapt Disraeli's reply to "What is your religion?" and answer "the religion of all cultivated people."

There is a further dimension to this. In the political and religious conflicts loosed on Europe by the Reformation, my intellectual judgment is nevertheless with the moderate Reformers—for that was the way to the future, a wider measure of freedom and toleration. So my judgment is not a matter of prejudice, but a reasoned one, which I am prepared to defend, in preferring Erasmus to Calvin or St. Ignatius, William the Silent to the Duke of Alva, Elizabeth I to Philip II, the Anglican Church to the Puritans.

This same option for aesthetic values, for a sensible skepticism and culture, the enjoyment of life in full, is that of the most distinguished cultural historian of our time—appropriately the biographer of Erasmus —Huizinga. But there is an analogous sense of the poetry, the heroism and pathos of life in the hearts of the best historians, in Macaulay and Froude, in Parkman and Prescott, even in the eighteenth-century Gibbon, as in two of our best twentieth-century historians, George Macaulay Trevelyan and Samuel Eliot Morison.

Finally, what about the responsibility of the scholar in regard to public affairs?

I do not know that the scholar has any special responsibility, over and above his duty as a citizen like any other, to speak out—much less lay down the law— about politics.

There seems to be an assumption—perhaps owing to the increasing dependence of our society upon experts—that expertise in one field qualifies a person to special attention in another. In fact it does not qualify him—sometimes it imposes a further disqualification. Take the notorious case of Bertrand Russell. My old friend G. M. Trevelyan, a Cambridge contemporary who knew Russell well over a lifetime, said to me: "He may be a genius at mathematics—as to that I am no judge; but he is a perfect goose about politics."

Russell's whole political record shows that that was true. In the First World War Britain and France were exhausted by 1917 and, after the collapse of Russia, could never have held out but for America coming into the war. When it was a question of Britain's very survival, this leading mathematician could only discern that the purpose of American troops being sent to Britain was to break strikes. Again, one would have to be very clever—or a great ass—to see only this in it. Russell published this statement and very properly was sent to prison for it.

The Russells are like the Bourbons in learning little, if at all, the hard way. Having been a conscientious objector in the first German war, Russell thought that resistance to Germany in the second was justified. If it was justified in the second, it was justified in the first, for both wars were but crests in the mounting wave of German determination to achieve world-power in this century—as the work of the leading German historian in the field today, Fritz Fischer's *Der Begriff an der Weltmacht*, makes crystal clear from all the evidence.

(The campaign of the historical "revisionists" after

the first German war, both in America and Britain, in undermining the peace settlement, played straight into the hands of those elements in Germany determined on another attempt, and in the event helped to pave the way to the second war.)

After the second, when it was clear that the expansionist aims of Soviet Russia were a threat to world peace, Russell publicly suggested a preventive nuclear bomb on Moscow. When later taxed with this, he admitted what could not be denied and said that he had forgotten he had ever urged it!

Suppose if some comparable Establishment figure had advocated anything so dastardly, suppose if Trevelyan or I had done—we should never have been allowed to forget it. The plain fact is that serious, intelligent people do not take the views of such a man on public affairs seriously. He would have done better to keep to his mathematics and philosophy, where he knew what he was talking about.

For there is an intellectual consideration of relevance here. Politics is concerned essentially with human beings in the mass, not with abstractions. It is a specific disqualification from understanding politics for one's mind to have been trained on abstractions, the abstractions of moral philosophy, let alone mathematics. Francis Bacon understood this well. George Santayana—whom Americans would do well to pay far more attention to—knew Russell intimately in earlier years and put his finger on the trouble quite early, before 1914:

> Bertrand Russell, on the whole, is not a very trustworthy thinker: he has the fault common to the political radicals of being disproportionately annoyed at things only slightly wrong or weak in others, and of flaming up into quite temporary enthusiasms for one panacea after another.

But there was something more deeply wrong. In a subsequent letter Santayana diagnosed:

> There is a strange mixture in him, as in his brother, of great ability and great disability; prodigious capacity and brilliance here—astonishing unconsciousness and want of perception there. They are like creatures of a species somewhat different from man.

I might add the point that brilliance in one specialized subject is liable to arrogance about other subjects where the scholar has no call to be heard. It is this arrogance, this assumption that they know better than the men on the job and carrying the burden, that so much irritates political leaders in intellectuals. In fact, intellectuals do not know better, they know less well; and often they are ignorant not only of the facts, the factors at work, the balance of forces, what is really at stake underneath the surface events, but they often display simple bad judgment, an incapacity to estimate the practical consequences of following out their line of thought to its disastrous conclusion. As if one can simply opt out of any human situation—let alone a world power out of a world-situation with impunity. There is total *ir*responsibility.

No wonder Catherine the Great, a highly intelligent woman, herself a good deal of an intellectual, a friend of Voltaire and Diderot, spoke with scorn of doctrinaire thinking about politics, as if things happened *"comme sur le papier qui souffre tout."*

An historian should know better and understand the world of politics and international affairs, for that is what his subject is about. And an historian—who deals in time—should, more than most intellectuals (mathematical logicians like Russell, for example), know how to be patient. Historians are frequently confronted in history with situations that are inextricable, that human beings are caught in and cannot help —as Jefferson himself found out, when he became President and was confronted by the intractable situation of Britain's life-and-death struggle with Napoleon. Even Jefferson had to admit that there was no good course to follow: there was only the choice between two evils. History may be said to have taught the rational philosopher a lesson. But, also, historians should know how little rational men are; in politics, even when there is a clear, right course to pursue, they often won't pursue it because of some private interest, some lobby they are engaged to, or simply out of personal dislike, some temperamental antipathy, or out of vanity, or egoism. Humans are only rarely rational.

We can adduce two cogent examples in our time of men who understood the historic trends of what was going on around them because they were historical-minded, their views firmly rooted in history. Of all British politicians Churchill knew what to expect of Germany and what would come from attempting to appease her—for he had been there before. That is one main advantage in the study of history—you can learn *vicariously*, without having to suffer it in your own hides all over again. He also knew, as optimistic leftists did not, what to expect from Soviet Russia—the long-term aims of a state do not alter for going through a promising revolution (especially when the promise and the hopes are not fulfilled).

As an historian Churchill was an amateur of genius; but our most influential professional historian, Sir Lewis Namier, was also proved right by events. He had the advantage of being a Continental, an Eastern European, a Polish Jew—so that he, too, knew exactly what to expect from Germany's record in the past century. Namier was so incisive a scholar that his book on the diplomatic prelude to the war, written before the documents from the archives were published, needed no essential revision when they were published. He had got it right beforehand—a remarkable example of historical perception.

But that historians can go wrong—you have only to consider the notorious case of Charles Beard. To judge from Beard's shocking book on the prelude to America's entry into the war, you would think that at Pearl Harbor it was the Americans who attacked the Japanese! We understand very well the personal reasons, the bias and sheer bad judgment that led this scholar astray—Samuel Eliot Morison dealt with him faithfully, if too kindly, in his celebrated essay, "The Shaving of a Beard." Morison, in his attitude toward public affairs, has displayed a steadiness of judgment, a width of understanding, a liberality and justice of mind, totally wanting in Beard. But then Morison is a great historian—I do not think that a good historian could go so far astray.

And it shows up the invalidity of much of Beard's earlier work, too, his interpretation of the making of the Constitution by the founding fathers in terms of a crude and cynical economic materialism, when in fact they were engaged in the most remarkable constructive work of the eighteenth century—making a new nation, and providing a framework to hold it together, by which it could operate and develop into an unknown future.

Let us conclude, then, that a further rule for the scholar to aim at, both in his own special work and in regard to public affairs, is *justice of mind.* It is in fact a rare quality—Abraham Lincoln had it in an exceptional degree. How rarely one finds it today, say, in literary criticism!—and yet criticism is of little value without it.

A vocational disease of scholars—especially of intellectuals—is to be the victims of words and phrases. They react emotionally to the thought of "power-politics," as they call it. But all politics is inevitably about power: what is the alternative? Would you have "weakness-politics," "debility-politics"? Common sense should tell one that one can hardly negotiate successfully from a position of weakness and abdication. That is the obvious way to be taken advantage of by the real devotees of power-politics, who practice and believe in nothing else.

The famous phrase, "All power corrupts," was coined by a scholar, an historian and a liberal, Lord Acton; everybody repeats it and, so far as I know, it has never been questioned. *But it is not true.* Power sometimes corrupts; but very often power improves a man—it widens his horizons and gives him a greater sense of responsibility. It depends on the man. Power made Napoleon drunk with it, and made Hitler mad —though he was evil enough before. But power made Abraham Lincoln, from being a provincial politician, into a statesman. And power turned Winston Churchill, from being a rather too volatile, too wilful and impulsive politician, into a responsible national leader. The possession of power properly weighted him down, gave him ballast, and kept him on the rails. Power never turned Queen Elizabeth I's head: it formed her into "a nursing mother of her people." It is largely a question of responsibility, whether power gives added responsibility with the burdens and experience it brings.

In regard to public affairs, no democratic government objects to responsible criticism—in fact, it needs it. But it must be *responsible*.

You may rightly ask: what is responsible criticism? Well, it is evidently not any criticism; it is not just an emotional, hysterical explosion without regard to consequences. Without regard to this consequence, for example, which Americans would do well to ponder over: forgive an outsider (but a well-wisher) for saying this, but an outsider sees more of the game.

Be careful, be cautious about attacking your own country: for whatever you say will be taken up, exaggerated, and made use of by your enemies abroad. There is no doubt from the evidence that the notorious resolution of the Oxford students in the 1930s that they would "not fight for King and Country" had an influence in Nazi Germany in encouraging Germans to think that Britain would not fight. (In the event, hundreds of Oxford students died fighting against Hitler.)

Responsible criticism is then: first, informed: it takes the trouble to find out the facts, it attempts seriously to weigh the factors and forces involved. Second, it is inspired with a constructive aim, not destructive, i.e., by the desire to help, to clarify the legitimate interests of your country—for they are fundamental to its existence and must be safeguarded—and then how far they coincide with or may be reconciled with the legitimate interests of other countries. That is the basis for international understanding and the comity of nations, the reconciliation of interests, providing properly for them—not just a hysterical skedaddle and scuttle, with disastrous consequences, leaving a situation worse than before.

One must always consider the consequences

It is obvious, I fear, that irresponsible intellectuals like Bertrand Russell rarely consider these; hence the disrepute they bring upon the name of "intellectual" among ordinary people, not only among practical men in public affairs but among people at large. Samuel Eliot Morison, in his great *History of the American People,* refers to "that contempt for intellect which is one of the unlovely traits of democracy everywhere"; and Richard Hofstadter devoted a whole book to the subject of anti-intellectualism in America.

But what if "intellectuals"—not necessarily, by the way, those possessing the best intellects—justify that contempt? Intellectuals should be particularly careful not to give cause to call forth anti-intellectualism by irresponsibility with regard to public affairs and public issues. They, above all people, should show a sense of responsibility, all the more so because they are distrusted by the ordinary Philistine.

Also for a more important reason. There has grown up a regrettable division, practically a gulf between the intellectuals as such and the nation at large. This is bad for both. Intellectuals should consent to learn the wisdom of experience; any craftsman needs to submit himself to the material he works in. Similarly we intellectuals, if we wish to make a useful contribution to public discussion, need to learn the necessary conditions that determine and limit political action—what Bismarck called *"le tact des choses possibles."* We need to learn ourselves before being so ready to tell others—who may, in fact, know more about the subject and its practical difficulties, sometimes its impossibilities.

Dean Acheson, certainly a powerful intellect, has written: "Intellectuals were quick and correct in pointing out that ultimate reality in foreign affairs was not found in terms of power alone. They were not always so quick to see that neither was it to be found in moral or political principle alone." It was Abraham Lincoln who warned against being misled by abstractions: he called them "pernicious abstractions" and the people who dealt in them "the scribblers."

To conclude, by contrast, with what *responsible* scholars, university people and intellectuals, can contribute in the realm of public affairs—allow me to cite some examples from my own University of Oxford, simply because I know it best.

When the great Cambridge scholar, F. W. Maitland, came over to deliver the Ford Lectures and chose for his subject the Town-fields of Cambridge, he apologised gracefully with "What fields has not Oxford made her own?"

Over the years I have watched a number of scholars who have made their contributions to public life, to political and international affairs, in the most responsible and constructive manner possible. And the significant thing is that they were the best, the leading scholars. Gilbert Murray was the most eminent Greek scholar of his age: he was one of the founders and upholders of the League of Nations. H. A. L. Fisher was a modern historian, who went into politics to become Minister of Education and promote the cause of "continuation-schools" for young people after the school-leaving age. Arnold Toynbee, Sir Lewis Namier, Sir George Clark, Sir Llewelyn Woodward, B. H. Sumner—all notable historians—served notably in the Royal Institute of International Affairs. A number of Oxford historians propagated the ideal of trusteeship for native races and undeveloped people within the Commonwealth. I can mention only Sir Reginald Coupland—historian of East Africa, Wilberforce and the Anti-Slavery Movement—who gave his best to the Royal Commisions on Palestine and on India, and his last energies to the crucial study of nationalities within the Commonwealth. There is the Australian historian, Sir Keith Hancock, biographer of Smuts, who, from being Britain's opponent in the South African war, became a foremost Commonwealth statesman. Dr. Margery Perham, in addition to her scholarly works, her standard biography of Lord Lugard—the administrator of Nigeria who, in his lifetime, kept it together in the spirit of trusteeship—has made herself a constant spokesman of the African peoples.

This circle, formed around the periodical, *The Round Table,* proved a training ground for younger scholars to make their contribution, in the proper spirit of responsibility, to public affairs. I believe that this is the right model for scholars to follow in their interventions in public matters: both responsible and constructive.

Perhaps in this series of lectures at Detroit, it may not be out of place to cite those examples from Oxford. After all, what fields has not Detroit made her own? You may say, with John Wesley, that the world is your parish.

3

The Historian and His Society: A Sociological Inquiry—Perhaps

BY J. H. HEXTER

Charles J. Stillé Professor of History, Yale University

Some years ago, Ved Mehta wrote for the *New Yorker Magazine* a series of articles on the practice of history. They were based on the views expressed to him by several eminent British historians, and reported with what accuracy who knows. Bearing the curious title "The Flight of the Crook-Taloned Birds," the articles seemed to demonstrate among other things—

1. that perhaps some English historians are unduly addicted to behaving in a fashion associated with a place on the other side of St. George's Channel called Donnybrook;

2. that English historians must be intrinsically more interesting than American historians, since the latter achieve notoriety only through the occupancy or pursuit of public office while the former seem to stumble into it just by being themselves;

3. that oral communication to an innocent-seeming Indian may not be the ideal means of formulating one's views on history for dissemination to a wider public.

What follows is an attempt to clean up only a small corner of the area that Mehta's broad brush so generously spattered. At one point he dealt with the views of E. H. Carr, expressed in a book called *What is History?* The title implies a modesty not wholly characteristic of the work itself, which with greater accuracy might have been entitled *What History Is*. As Mehta puts it, "In his book, Carr unhesitatingly held on to his belief—'that all history is relative to the historians who write it, and all historians are relative to their historical and social background.'" "Quoting Mr. Carr ('Before you study the history, study the historian. . . . Before you study the historian, study his historical and social environment.'), history was not objective (possessing a hard core of facts) but subjective (possessing a hard core of interpretation). Each generation reinterpreted history to suit itself. . . ." So much for Ved Mehta. We might add another posy to the bouquet of quotations from Carr.

When "we take up a work of history our first concern should be not with the facts which it contains but with the historian who wrote it." The onetime shepherd of all historians in the United States, Dr. Boyd Shafer, former executive secretary of the American Historical Association and editor of the *American Historical Review*, instructed his flock that Carr's *What Is History?* was "the best recent book in English on the nature of historical study."[1] We historians then were practically bound by pastoral injunction to browse in the intellectual meadow that Carr had so generously provided us. Already, perhaps the reader

1. *American Historical Review* 67 (1962): 676.

may have inferred that I am in something less than perfect sympathy not only with the judgment of Dr. Shafer but with the statements of Carr, and with the point of view which they enfold. In this he would be correct.

Carr has formulated that point in another way. You cannot "fully understand or appreciate the work of the historian, unless you have first grasped the standpoint from which he himself approached it." Thus he says, in order fully to understand his *History of Rome*, one must know about Theodor Mommsen's disillusionment with the liberal revolution of 1848. Fully to understand his *England under Queen Anne* one must know that George Macaulay Trevelyan was "the last of the great liberal historians of the Whig tradition;" fully to understand his *The Structure of Politics at the Accession of George III*, one must know that Lewis Namier was a continental conservative.[2] At this point in Carr's disquisition, I ground to an abrupt halt. It suddenly struck me that there were two early American Namierites, and that by a wild coincidence they were among the historians whom I had known best and longest.

The first is Professor Walcott, whom I have

2. E. H. Carr, *What Is History?* (New York: Knopf, 1965), pp. 24–48.

known for thirty-five years; the second is myself whom I have known for a bit longer. Professor Walcott is a Namierite by choice; and I had watched with awe the incipient Namierization of the early Parliament of the eighteenth century from close in, when we occupied neighboring stalls in Widener Library. I am a Namierite by grace of a reviewer for *The Economist* who has admitted me to "the nuclear club whose first member was Sir Lewis Namier."

Since we were both charter members of the Harvard Chapter of the Teachers' Union back in the 30s, I take it that during his early Namierizing days, Professor Walcott was not a conservative. And, born in Cambridge, Massachusetts, he is a continental only in the eighteenth-century American, not in the British sense of the word. As for myself, I was once a member of the Grievance Committee of the red-infested New York College Chapter of that same Teachers' Union, and of four academic colleagues who were invited to my wedding, three subsequently took the Fifth Amendment in the course of loyalty investigations. And I am not a continental either. I am a Cincinnatian. Now if to understand Professor Namier's history it is important to know that he was a continental conservative, to understand our writing is it equally important to know that Professor Walcott and I, two early Namierites, were *not* continental conservatives

—or even just conservatives. If Namier's attitude toward society is the first thing that readers of his work need to know, what effect did my *ignorance* of his attitude have on me back in the thirties when, scarcely conscious of the fact, I became a Namierite?

And this brings us to another puzzle. Why should Professor Namier's politics strike Carr, no Namierite, as important, and me, a Namierite, as unimportant? The difference lies in the question Carr and I are interested in finding answers to. Carr wants to know why Namier wrote a book like *The Structure of Politics at the Accession of George III.* For people with a taste for this sort of guessing game, amateur seat-of-the-pants psychologizing is less a vice than an unfortunate but inevitable consequence of raising the problem in the first place. I know this because I have had a try at the game myself in connection with Thomas More's *Utopia.* My early questions about *The Structure of Politics* were of a character very different from Carr's. They were as follows:

1. What that is new does the book say about English politics in the middle of the eighteenth century?

2. Has it got the story right?

3. Can I make any use of the way *The Structure of Politics* was put together in the kind of work I am doing?

Suppose I had put those questions to Carr, and he had

replied, "When you take up *The Structure of Politics,* your first concern is to know that Lewis Namier was a continental conservative." I fear my reply would have been, "I can with difficulty conceive a less relevant answer to my questions."

Carr has stated his purpose in another way. It is "to show how closely the work of the historian mirrors the society in which he works." Now, if by the society in which he works, Carr means the vast tumultuous event-matrix of all human happenings during his lifetime, then like everybody else the historian mirrors it badly, because only a very small part if it can ever be in any one man's range of perception. The sector of human happenings a man is likely to mirror best is the one he is involved in most, the society or societies, the associations of men, in which he indeed lives and works.

We need not embark on an arduous and uncertain quest for the society in which historians work. With great wisdom and perceptiveness it has been identified for us by the federal government; and annually the Internal Revenue Service reminds us of the facts of life. Crushed and bleeding from the embrace of the Iron Maiden, Form 1040, we seek among the cancelled checks for some surcease from pain, and we find: dues, American Historical Association; dues,

Organization of American Historians; dues, Economic History Society; dues, Renaissance Society—deductible. Expenses: meeting of Midwest Conference on British Historical Studies—deductible. Subscription, *Journal of Modern History*—deductible; subscription, *History and Theory*—deductible. Depreciation of library, almost all history books—deductible. Share of utilities for space used in the house for writing history—deductible. The United States Government then has not a moment's doubt about what society I work in. It says that I work in the society of professional historians. And as a neighbor of mine used to remark, "What's good enough for Uncle Sam is good enough for me."

An inordinate amount of what has been said about historians and the history they write has gotten into stultifying tangles because no heed has been paid to the fact that preeminently the society which professional historians are members of, belong to, work in, is the society of professional historians. Nearly all the competent history writing done nowadays is done by professional historians, people who are trained in and live by the regular practice of history as lawyers live by the practice of law, physicians by the practice of medicine. In these matters the very first line historians draw is the one that separated the particular community of professionals from the rest of the world who with respect to law or medicine or history are lay-men. Yet in face of the massive professionalization of the writing of history, most people who have medi-tated publicly on the way history gets written have not seen fit to make any analysis, much less to make a serious investigation, of the effect on historians of their membership in a society of professionals. What I would like to do here is to suggest a few of the conse-quences of membership.

The most important consequence of entry into the society of historians is that the entrant is thereafter called upon to write history. To get history written is the only unique purpose of the society, the only trait that unmistakably distinguishes it from other similar societies. To get history written, not to get it taught. Academia itself usually makes teaching a condition of employment for professional historians, and since there are few other paying posts available to them, they teach willy-nilly, usually willy, but sometimes nilly.

The central institution of the society of historians is judgment by peers. He who enters the society of pro-fessional historians thereafter subjects himself to the judgment of the other accredited members of that so-ciety. This process of judgment determines the rela-tion of the individual historian to that society which more than any other affects his chosen life work. It imposes on the varied individuals who are members of the society a common discipline by precept, and the other institutions of the society enforce that discipline.

One trait of judgment by historical peers sharply differentiates it from such judgment in the courts of law. The latter kind of judgment forbids double jeopardy. A verdict in favor of a man brought to trial on charges before his peers in a court of law is not subject to reversal at any future time by any authority whatsoever. The society of historians acts on a rule diametrically opposite to this—a principle of multiple jeopardy and unlimited reversal. At any time any historian may subject the life work or any fragment of the life work of any other historian to a judgment, and no statute of limitations runs against him. (Thucydides has recently got into bad trouble.) The historian puts himself forever at the mercy of the present and future members of his society each time he emerges from the enclosed comfortable womb of silence into the cold clattering public marketplace of print.

The subjection of what one writes to judgment by one's peers is not often pleasant, and the temptation to avoid it is strong. By not writing at all one can avoid it. But since the main object of the society of historians is to see to it that history gets written, it cannot tolerate evasion of this sort. To prevent it, the society in which historians work has adopted another institution of the English common law. Rather early, that law had to cope with an analogous problem. Unless a man would plead to the charges against him before his peers, he could not be judged.

To avoid the awkward consequences of this situation the common law employed a device called *peine forte et dure.* The *peine* was provided by weights which were piled on the recalcitrant to persuade him to face judgment. If he persisted in his obduracy, weights continued to be added until he either changed his mind or was crushed to death. The society of historians in its infinite wisdom has so arranged matters that the effective alternative to publishing and facing the judgment of one's peers is to be crushed to death professionally by the weight of their indifference. So for the historian, too, it is "plead or die," or in another aphorism "publish or perish." Of course, just as the man before the bar of justice may plead *and* be condemned, it is not at all unlikely that a historian will publish *and* perish; still the odds, however unfavorable, are better than no chance at all, and for the man who never publishes there is no chance at all.

The mechanisms of judgment by peers in the society of historians are numerous and varied, formal and informal, public and private, written and oral. We can deal only briefly with a few of these mechanisms.

It is, of course, in the learned journals that we find the most conspicuous and noisy mechanism for judgment—the book review section. Also most formal, most formidable and most effective in the short run, but, unfortunately, perhaps the least accurate and the least competent. Why formal reviewing in the learned journals of the historical profession in America is pretty bad would take long to explain, because part of the badness is rooted in the very structure of the craft, while another part is related to the character or rather a few characteristics, of American society as a whole. A third part of the badness is the result of remediable operating deficiencies of the professional journals which could (but probably will not) be corrected with inconvenience only to the editors of those journals.

One or two of the more obvious defects of the review columns of the journals as channels for judgment by peers, however, need to be mentioned. In the first place they move too fast. To a novice historian who with bated breath waits for two years after publication for the first review of his book, the notion that judgment comes too fast will seem ludicrous. What usually delays the review, however, is not the reviewer's deep thinking about the book, but his avoidance of thinking and writing at all about a book concerning which he does not feel he has anything sensible to say, or his mere laziness and insouciance. Moreover there are more reviewing journals than there are willing and able reviewers. Reviewing is an exacting, time-consuming, ill-rewarded skill likely to win the reviewer more enemies than friends, rarely undertaken by senior members of the society except as a favor to a friend, as part of a brawl with an old opponent, or more properly and I suspect more frequently as a part payment of the non-economic dues they owe their profession. Finally the journals review only books, never an article, no matter how important that article may be. Nonetheless and despite the drawbacks and deficiencies of reviewing, the society of historians needs an evaluation however tentative of the output of its members, and the writing historian for professional, practical and psychological reasons does not want to wait indefinitely for the first shower of roses and/or dead cats.

Even before the long slow drizzle of reviews of a book is over, the more loosely-structured and, be it said, more reliable judgment by peers starts; and in the case of articles these judgments are the earliest ones. A useful formal and public mechanism of this kind of judgment is the footnote. It is a splendid and versatile instrument which serves many purposes besides its ostensible one—that of indicating where an author claims to find support for a statement. Among these purposes is the provision of a convenient location for the payment of scholarly debts. The instru-

ment of payment is not in its form quite as fully stand-
ardized as ordinary commercial instruments, but it
usually goes something like "For a fuller discussion of
the above point see Wallaby's solid article 'The De-
cline of Possum Hunting in Dade County as a Crite-
rion of Evangelical Revival,' *The Florida Journal of
History*, 12(1947), 12–17. Robert Ryerson's *The Possum as a Frontier Phenomenon: Myth and Reality*
(Madison, Wis., 1959) is too general and too unrelia-
ble for use." The last part of the above footnote carries
its own warning. Those little devices are not merely
organs of praise but instruments of judgment, and woe
is the miscreant bore who had inflicted his incompetence on an irascible judge with a footnote handy
to hang him on.

Academic correspondence provides a private, indeed confidential, but highly effective mechanism of
judgment. For example, in answer to an inquiry Professor A. receives the following letter from Professor
B., whom on other like occasions has proved to be a
reliable source of information. "In connection with the
opening you mention in Early Modern History, I have
a few suggestions. They do not include Adcock, about
whom you specifically ask me. His recent articles suggest that he is very suitably placed in his present job
at Grand Guignot State Teachers."

The life of the professional historian is the life of

teaching, silent study, work, and writing, interspersed with brief orgies of gossip. According to Adam Smith, where two or three businessmen gather, there is a conspiracy in restraint of trade. According to the apostle, where two or three gather in faith, there is the church. Where two or three historians gather, there is gossip. Where there is gossip there is shop talk, and where there is shop talk there is judgment by peers. It goes on on the steps of Sterling or Widener or the New York Public Library or the National Archives or the British Museum or the Bibliothèque Nationale. It goes on among members of the same department, and it goes on with somewhat enhanced intensity in those innumerable meetings of groups with a shared specialization into which the society of professional historians finds it convenient to fracture itself—the Central States Renaissance Conference, the History of Science Society, the Conference on British Studies, and so on. Here is just one very brief sample to show how it works:

"I have been so swamped with chores this semester I haven't had a look at Frisbie's new book on the Scottish Parliaments."
"Don't bother."

The crucial judgments are considerably less casual, and the most careful and painstaking of them take place in the confidential deliberations of *ad hoc* committees and departments of history dealing with appointments and promotions. The better the department the more careful and penetrating the judgment. This I have reason to know because it is my good fortune currently to be a member of the Department of History at Yale University, a group of historians committed by preference and required by circumstance to render judgment on one peer or another rather often. I remember vividly a meeting of the department's permanent officers, its tenured members, some years ago. Should the department meet an offer made to one of its able young members from another university by promoting him to a position that gave him tenure? The small committee which had read all his published work and a manuscript that he was ready to submit to a publisher came in with a split vote. Other members had also done some reading. After two hours of wholly unacrimonious debate, it was evident that the decision would rest on a judgment of the manuscript. "Well," a former president of the American Historical Association said wearily, "it looks like we have to go and do some more homework." So over the next two weeks some twenty-five of the better-paid members of the profession spent a very considerable number of man-hours reading the manuscript and arriving at their tentative individual judgments. They then met again for two more hours of deliberation before coming to their collective judgment. Thank God, judgment is not always, or even often, that expensive, difficult, and time-consuming.

As a structured entity the machinery of judgment by peers in our society is awesome; I can imagine that, called to admire its elaborate convolutions, however, some crude iconoclast might ask what purposes of any sort it serves. It serves as the foundation of two other primary institutions of our society. In the first place it establishes the pecking order. It operates as a rating device and develops a consensus among historians as to who's who and about how who he is.[3]

The pecking order along with the movements of demand determines the going prices of particular historians on the job market. To a considerable extent it determines what according to one's rhetorical preference may be called the allocation of the conventional rewards of academia, the apportionment of distributive justice, who gets how big a piece of pie, or the division of the loot. There are, of course, other means, some proper and useful, some sordid, for augmenting the conventional rewards of academia, but probably the surest over the long run is to write history favora-

3. For a more broadly based inquiry into the function of publication, see J. H. Hexter, "Publish or Perish—A Defense," *The Public Interest,* 17 (1969): 60–77.

bly judged by one's peers. Granting exceptions, most of the cushier posts in history's corner of academia are in the hands of historians deemed by their peers to have written competent history.

But—one can almost hear the pathetic sob—what of the dedicated teacher? The question is raised frequently—one who has heard it again and again may be inclined to say, *ad nauseam*. It has often been alleged that in the dealing out of loaves and fishes, the provision of distributive justice, the apportioning of the conventional rewards averted to above, our society, the society of historians commits chronic and grave injustice by overrewarding the productive scholar who cannot teach for beans, and underrewarding the gifted teacher who does not—this last to be said with an appropriately contemptuous curling of the lips—"grind out research." This view of the situation depends on a number of assumptions no less nonsensical for being almost universally accepted, one or two accepted indeed by the very research scholars who are their intended victims, and who having assented to a false assumption find themselves logically pressed toward conclusions that they know are absurd. An assumption of this last kind is the one which equates teaching with classroom performance, and in its most extreme form with performance before a group of students of considerable size. This odd equation, reflected in the statement I once heard made about an eminent scholar, "He is good in seminars, but he can't teach," is too foolish to waste powder and shot on.

It is the more moderate view, the view that all important teaching is done in the presence of pupils, that enjoys almost universal approval. Of course, to define teaching as the transmission of knowledge and understanding by word of mouth in face-to-face relation between pedagog and pupils may be convenient for some purposes, especially perhaps for the purposes of persons who transmit knowledge and understanding in no other way. Nevertheless, five hundred years after Herr Gutenberg's entertaining invention such a definition has a somewhat archaic aroma. There are three major formal means by which historical understanding and knowledge are in fact transmitted to those who seek knowledge and understanding: 1) the reading of sources, 2) the reading of what historians have written about the sources and about the works of other historians they have read, and 3) the hearing of talk by historians in which they purvey whatever knowledge they have acquired through their own reading of sources and of what other historians have said about those sources. It seems to me highly probable that most people with any considerable amount of historical knowledge and depth of historical understanding owe the larger part of both to what they have read by historians rather than to what they have heard from them.

But surely, it may be said, the dedicated teacher who has a block about writing ought to receive rewards equal to, perhaps superior to, the man who publishes a bit and has a block about teaching a class. Since the issue is cast in terms of ethical imperatives rather than of actualities we can avoid dealing with the implication, quite possibly contrary to fact, that all the goodies, psychological and material, are showered on research historians, who are bad teachers, while the devoted teachers, who are not research historians, stand out in the cold, their pitiful pinched faces pressed against the window pane. But we must at least indicate that the proponents of the "dedicated teacher" canard have won a handsome propaganda victory. Somehow in certain circles they have put across the idea that practically all historians who do competent scholarly work are maundering bores in the classroom, and that they treat their students like gnats, to be brushed off or, if the students are persistent and the professor short-tempered, like mosquitoes to be slapped at. Conversely, the mere fact that a college teacher of history has published nothing is somehow transformed into *prima facie* evidence that he is so profoundly involved in teaching that he has no time to spare for turning out trifles in the research line. Unfortunately for its propagators this view has made relatively little headway in the society of historians, because the leaders of that society know it is pure poppycock. In the course of their careers they have known too many superb teaching historians (we here follow without accepting the usage which confines the term teaching to a face-to-face relation), who, stinting nothing in their classrooms or in their concern for their students, have yet done scholarly work of distinction. They have also known colleagues who published nothing, not because of their devotion to teaching but because of their whole-hearted dedication to birdwatching, to billiards, to Old Overholt, to squalid in-fighting on the lower rungs of the ladder of academic politics, or simply to providing their backsides with facilities for acquiring an appropriate middle-age spread. Despite its well-nigh universal rejection at the better addresses in academia, the peculiar myth that hopefully we have just buried has long flourished in some academic circles and is propagated with unchecked fungoid luxuriance in the shady academic demimonde inhabited by educationists whose dim view of research and scholarship is doubtless an undistorted reflection of the quality of their own professional publications.

One last fallacy of the justice-for-devoted-teachers crusade (which, as often happens in crusades, occasionally nudges over into a witch hunt against the advancement of learning) needs to be dealt with. It is necessary to admit that some men who write good history are bad classroom teachers. Yet they are judged by their peers as good historians. But does not equity then demand that the successful classroom performer who cannot write history also be judged as a good historian and enjoy thereby all the rights, privileges, honors and honoraria thereto appurtent? Let us examine this apparently equitable proposal more closely. How do we know whether the man who writes history is a competent historian? We know, because he has taken the pains to provide us with clear evidence readily and publicly accessible. If he who runs cannot read, at least he who will sit down for a few hours can read—and judge. The historian who writes can be judged on the basis of standards that have been set by the collective experience of his peers and by the achievements of the ablest members of the society of which he is a member. Who judges the competence of the classroom teacher as an historian, and by what standards is he judged? In the main he is judged by the undergraduate students who listen to his lectures, and by what standards God only knows.

We do know, however, if we will but recollect our own undergraduate days, how little our standards had to do with the teacher's competence as an historian. Is there one of us who does not recall having been enthralled in our early college years by a classroom teacher of history whom we later discovered to be a pretentious faker or a mere clown—*vox et praeterea nihil?* I was neither the dullest nor the most easily excited of undergraduates; but in my second year in college I was profoundly impressed by a teacher of history, by her wit, her urbanity, by her way of talking about Charlemagne, and Innocent III, and Robespierre, as if they were ordinary fellows who lived right down the block. By my third year I had rightly come to regard this same teacher as an utter fraud. This provides us perhaps with some clue as to the reliability of that indirect evidence on which historians mainly judge the pedagogic merits of their fellows. In this case the evidence is of the kind that the more exacting judges are inclined to deem most reliable—the opinions of an "A" student. In this instance in the space of one year the opinions of one "A" student would have provided wholly contradictory evidence about the same teacher. If in judging their peers the society of historians is inclined to have greater confidence in the kind of evidence that a colleague's writing puts in their reach than in the kind that his classroom teaching puts in their reach, it may not only be charitable but just to ascribe their preference to a sound evaluation of the quality of the evidence rather than to a dark conspiracy against competent classroom teachers. After all, aptitude in gauging the quality of evidence is one of the most highly treasured tricks of the historians' trade.

Moreover, traits in no way germane to a man's ability as an historian may and sometimes do diminish his effectiveness in the classroom. He may have a high whining voice; he may be extremely awkward; he may not be a ready improviser; he may have an incurable and severe stammer; he may be terribly shy; he may be deaf and so on. If severe enough and numerous enough, such traits may disqualify a man altogether from classroom teaching; but they all speak entirely to his aptitude for ready oral communication and not at all to his skill as an historian. On the other hand, it is hard to see what equivalent obstacles, immaterial to a man's competence as an historian, intervene to block the passage from spoken to written discourse. Surely there is no less need in oral than in written discourse for data coherently organized, relevant, and enlightening. And such a need is no less pressing in the *viva voce* than in the written communication of history. Therefore, anyone who speaks history as it should be spoken ought to be able to write history as it should be written. Something of course may be lost in the writing—the pregnant pause, the ironic inflection, the delicate shrug, the telling gesture, the raised eyebrow. Still with the exercise of a little ingenuity verbal surrogates for these varieties of vocal and physical twitching can occasionally be found. And on the balance while not denying that some of the meat of the spoken discourse may be lost when it gets set down in cold print, one occasionally wonders whether the meat in question is roast beef or ham. So much for the dedicated teacher of history who never writes history.

Our peers in the society of historians then judge us by what we write and subject to *peine forte et dure* those, even the non-writing dedicated teachers, who refuse to produce any testimony on which those peers can base a judgment. Thereby the society aims to apportion the conventional rewards of academia in some more or less sensible relation to the quality-cum-quantity of an historian's published work. Presumably this is the way the society to which we belong provides us with incentives to do our job, which is to get history written.

Incentives, however, are only important where the work to be done is dull and unrewarding, but historical research and writing . . . ! A swimming eye and an enraptured set of the face becomes practically mandatory as Parnassus heaves into view with the Muses draped along its slopes and Clio herself doing *entrechats* at the apex. It is a might pretty picture, but that is all it is.

A great deal of historical research and writing is stiflingly dull and unrewarding work. The vision of the historian as a sort of intellectual private eye, swashbuckling through a succession of unremittingly fascinating adventures of the mind, can survive only among those who do not destroy it by engaging in historical research. In fact a great deal of historical work is indeed like detective work, like the dreary, patient, systematic, interminable detective work that goes on in dozens of precincts and police headquarters—following dim leads down cold trails to dead ends, just in case; compiling large, uninteresting and frequently irrelevant dossiers; and questioning dreary and dull sources of information who (or which) often provide not an additional fragment of a clue to what one knows already.

If throughout this harrowing grind our historian has continuously burned with a hard gemlike flame, it is only because God endowed him more generously than He has endowed most men and most historians with the fuel of enthusiasm. Take a stroll some day where the historical researchers congregate in a great library. Note the number of scholars bowed over their desks, their heads resting on their arms. They are not at the moment burning with a hard gemlike flame;

they are not thinking deep and exciting thoughts; they are sleeping off their ennui. Their task—the task of historical scholarship—has bored them not to extinction, but to a merciful though temporary oblivion.

Still the research ends, the working up of the evidence into a finished piece of history writing starts, and the historian at last tastes the pleasure of scholarly creation. Or does he? Well, if he has an aptitude at the management of evidence and a flare for vigorous prose, perhaps he does enjoy himself a good bit. But what if he has not? Then through sheet after sheet of manuscript, past twisted sentences, past contorted paragraphs, past one pitiful wreck of a chapter after another he drags the leaden weight of his club-footed prose. Let us draw a curtain to blot out this harrowing scene and turn to look at one of the fortunate few to whom the writing of an historical study is a pleasure of sorts. He writes the last word of his manuscript with a gay flourish—and he better had, because it is the last gay flourish he is going to be able to indulge in for quite a while. He has arrived at the grey morning-after of historical scholarship, the time of the *katzen-jammer* with the old cigar butts and stale whisky of his recent intellectual binge still to be tidied up. He must reread the manuscript and then read the type-script and correct and revise as he reads. And he must, of course, check the quotations for accuracy of transcription and all the footnotes for accuracy of citation. Then he sends the fruit of this labor to a publisher; and if he is lucky, the publisher accepts it, asking only a thousand dollars or so by way of subvention to cover the cost of printing. In return for this benefaction the historian gets to read his handwork again in galley proof and yet again in page proof. And then comes the crowning indignity, when sick to death of his own best effort, he drains the nauseating dregs of historical scholarship; he has to read the damn thing again and prepare an index.

And then? And then judgment by peers. For the unfortunate on whom the verdict is unfavorable, any connoisseur of the review columns of the historical journals knows the delights in store for him. "Dr. Thompson has thrown new light—but not much of it —on one of the more trivial episodes in Italian diplomatic history." "Unfortunately Dr. Thompson has not taken the trouble to familiarize himself with the latest studies on this problem by Swedish scholars." "Dr. Thompson has not chosen to mention my study of Bergamese diplomatic documents, which perhaps he has not thought it worth the trouble to examine." "For an adequate treatment of Dr. Thompson's subject we will still perforce rely on the five magisterial tomes of

Colavito and Gentile published in the 1820s." "Thompson's rather bold and unorthodox view on certain personal eccentricities of Adolfo V, the so-called Mad Duke, are by no means sustained in the more cautious and conservative studies of Best-Chetwynd, F. Hill, Spillane, and de Sade." And so on, as one undergoes the capriciously-timed drip-drip of reviews in the historians' society's version of the Chinese water torture. Under these circumstances the society of historians wisely hangs on to the stick of *peine forte et dure* and the doughnut of the pecking order to keep its balky members pacing the treadmill that grinds out historical research.

Those who cannot contemplate with equanimity the foregoing account of how the wheels of productive historical scholarship are kept in motion would argue that history produced under conditions of labor rather like those of the more satanic early nineteenth-century textile mills will be worthless. Can men with little taste for historical work really do anything worthwhile? The answer to this question is "yes." The notion may not make happy those generous souls who, confusing their wishes with actuality, believe that competence waits on dedication. It does not. There are lovable, enthusiastic, and inept oafs in our profession, and there are deplorable, nonchalant, and skillful idlers. When the latter are routed out of their sacks and driven to labor in the vineyard, they always beat the former hands down in the judgment of their peers.

Readers who have not been distracted by the rhetorical arabesques of the foregoing from their effort to keep clear the lines of argument may have noticed some traces of ambiguity and equivocation. The central purpose of the society of historians, it was pointed out, was to see to it that history got written. The function of judgment by peers was to establish a pecking order for the purpose of facilitating distributive justice. And the purpose of differential distribution of the loot was to hold before historians the prospect of material reward in order to persuade them to dig hard at writing history. Thus judgment by peers was made to seem one of the mechanisms in an integrated series all directed toward maximizing quality and quantity of historical output. Somewhat closer scrutiny has indicated that this is not a very accurate account. Quite evidently in the matter of encouraging historical scholarship, the pecking order and the allocation of rewards are on the opposite side of the account from judgment by peers. By its terrors the latter prospect discourages publication. Hopefully the pecking order and the prospect of a good share of the loot offset the damage that judgment by peers has done. They work with it only in the misleading sense that

an antidote may be said to work with its correspond-
ing poison. Taken alone judgment by peers does not
stimulate the production of historical scholarship; it
retards and strangles it.

Then if the purpose of the society of professsional
historians is merely to get history written, the sensible
thing to do is to drop judgment by professional peers
altogether. This would not, of course, necessitate giv-
ing up the real stimuli to writing history. We would
retain *peine forte et dure*, the pecking order, and the
differential division of the conventional academic
rewards. We would even retain judgment. Only the
judges would not be an historian's professional peers.
Republican historians would write history for Republicans, to be judged by Republicans; organic garden-
ing historians would write history for organic gardeners to be judged by organic gardeners, and so on,
and we would hire a statistician, an econometrist and
a theory-of-games man to solve the problem of slicing
the pie.

Yet even though the incentive system just out-
lined would almost certainly release a great flood of
historical writing, it is doubtful that the society to
which historians belong would be willing to settle for
it. Despite the fact that judgment by peers dams in-
stead of releases that flood, the society of historians
will, I suspect, cling to that institution to which all the

rest are geared, and since it inhibits historians from writing, our earlier statement, "The purpose of the society of professional historians is to see to it that history gets written" is incomplete. Completing it is easy enough. One simply adds three words: the purpose of the society of historians is to see to it that history gets written *the right way*. In context "the right way" means "the way our society wants history written."

Although a rough consensus of the society of historians about the details of the right way to write history in fact exists, to describe and explain that consensus would take a good while. There is no doubt, however, as to the common opinion of our society about the *goal* of the right way. We want history written so that any one who wants to know anything knowable about the past can find it out; so that where knowledge is possible, it will also be present; so that wherever one seeks footing in the past, there will be as much footing and as solid footing as the careful, patient, and imaginative study of the surviving remnants of the past by men skilled in their craft can make available. It is to just one end that our society maintains its elaborate structure of *peine forte et dure*, judgment of peers, the pecking order, and the differential division of the rewards: that with the exercise of reasonable care and prudence whoever chooses to move about anywhere in the recorded past can find solid ground and not continually be tumbling into bogs, quicksand, crevasses, and pitfalls.

A couple of specific illustrations of the force of the rules of game—the guild standards, if you will— on professional practices and judgments of professional historians may serve better than general allegations to demonstrate the way the society of historians polices its members. The first illustration concerns a young scholar, Professor Jesse Lemisch, who proclaims himself a radical historian. He has recently published "Radical Plot in Boston (1770): A Study in the Use of Evidence," a twenty-page review of Hiller Zobel's *The Boston Massacre.*[4] Professor Lemisch's view is unfavorable to the book. He charges Zobel with "proof by dint of no evidence or contradictory evidence." Zobel argues, for example, that the mob in Boston was " 'controlled but in appearance unchecked.' " Yet according to Lemisch, the evidence says nothing of control and an abundance about excessive spontaneity. Further, he says, "Zobel consistently avoids evidence against his case." His case being that the Boston mob was manipulated, he fails to follow up clues, imbedded in the evidence which he himself offers, that some of the Boston rioters were moved by a genuine sense of grievance, indeed perhaps by genuine grievances against

4. *Harvard Law Review,* 84 (1970–71): 485–504.

the British troops. What he does with respect to the Boston mob he also does to the colonial leaders. He indulges in selective quotation. Thus John Adams was seriously alarmed at what, in his own words, he construed as "the determination in Great Britain to subjugate us" by military occupation. Only by omitting that quotation can Zobel maintain the credibility of his characterization of Adams's reaction: " 'in annoyance,' " he says. Further, Zobel's " 'positive identification' " of rioters in 1765 is based on "information from indictments—to which the accused plead not guilty and were never tried—for a riot which took place" during 1764. And so on.

From a reading of the review, two points to our purpose emerge clearly. First, Zobel takes a view of the behavior of the American colonials slightly more jaundiced than that of George III, and some of Lemisch's animus in the review results from ideological hostility to a historical perception different from his own, and averse to it. This is clear from some of his asides, such as:

> Can the lawyer [Zobel] draw from his studies of the preliminaries of a past American revolution no better "lesson" . . . than obedience, authority, the hard line . . . ? It may be appropriate to remind the reader at this point that in the years following the Massacre

such policies carried out by the people whom Zobel admires and on whom he relies for the greater part of his evidence precipitated revolution.[5]

With serious qualifying additions and amendments, I happen to draw from the recent "youth revolution" in the United States substantially the lesson of "obedience, authority, the hard line," which Lemisch finds lamentable. Moreover, in Lemisch's case casually and accidentally I have followed E. H. Carr's injunction, "Before you study the history, study the historian." Having done so, as a student of the sociology of knowledge, I can then understand Lemisch's review of Zobel's book as a manifestation of youthful academic malaise in the late 1960s and the early 1970s.

But second, with respect to the society of the sociologists of knowledge, I am a mere outsider. It is not the society I belong to. I belong to the society of historians, and my membership in it requires me to attend not to Lemisch's current sociopolitical postures in 1971, which I think will be ephemeral and which do not especially interest me, but to the substance of his criticism of a book about 1770. That substance, what Lemisch says about the uses of dubious evidence and loaded language, seems to me to leave Zobel with

5. *Ibid.,* p. 504. In the review the last sentence quoted above appears as a footnote.

a good many tough questions to answer. If he cannot answer them, he or someone else will have to modify his account of the Boston Massacre not to satisfy radical historians, but to satisfy historians. That is what makes the note Professor Lemisch wrote on the copy of the review he kindly sent me almost touchingly wrong-headed:

For Jack Hexter,
  from a radical asking some conservative questions about evidence and proof . . .

The whole implication of Lemisch's review is that there are no such things as radical or conservative questions about evidence and proof. Historical evidence is slight or abundant, dubious or trustworthy. Historical proof is difficult or easy, adequate or inadequate. Evidence and proof are never radical or conservative. Rather, they are part of the common language in which historians communicate with each other, the common ground on which they stand or fall. They are part of the discipline which, soon or late, the society of historians imposes on *all* its members.

The second illustration comes from a recent controversy in the historical journal *Past and Present.*[6] In

6. 44 (Aug., 1969): 52–75; 47 (May, 1970): 116–46.

an article entitled "The Presbyterian Independents Exorcised" a young American historian, Stephen Foster, impugned not the conclusions but the evidential base of another article published thirty years earlier on the political-religious alignments in Parliament during the English Civil War of the 1640s. Foster's article was 23 pages long. A subsequent issue of *Past and Present* carried five ripostes to Foster's argument and his rejoinder. They took up 30 pages. The five letters raised questions about the worth of Foster's evidence. Several of the writers returned fire to potshots that Foster had taken at some of their published views on religion and politics during the Civil War. He was even censured for American provincialism. Not the twentieth century, U.S. variety, however, but as a colonial historian, for the seventeenth-century Massachusetts Bay variety. He was charged with misconstruing some of his evidence because he had in mind the scene in New England rather than in old England. No critic tried to reconstruct Foster's *psyche* or *socii;* he was neither psychologized nor sociologized by his adversaries. Nor had he done the like to the historian whose thirty-year old work he challenged. Under the circumstances and given the issues, explorations of the singularities of Pearl and Foster, Hexter, Underhill, Worden, and Yule would have been felt as impertinent in both senses of the term both by the participants in the controversy and by the audience. Participants and audience alike, whatever their singularities, had one thing in common. They were members of the same society, the society of professional historians. The participants knew they were subject to the judgment of their peers in that society and, moreover, had in the course of their training internalized its values, and they behaved accordingly. They showed grounds for devaluating evidence previously adduced, offered evidence not hitherto brought forward, and argued alternate possible construals of the evidence available. And they felt that that was enough.

All this was just history—business-as-usual, not very important—and, except to the participants, not very interesting. And that, of course, is the trouble. In a ghastly way historians bouncing ideologies off each other are fascinating. In a low-comedy way so are historians who chase preconceptions and fall flat on their faces because in their haste they overlook the piece of evidence that trips them up. So naturally their sort of performance attracts attention. Moreover most very good historians have off and on slipped up this way either in the judgment of evidence or in the emission of *obiter dicta;* and lesser lights naturally derive spiritual solace from dwelling on what boobs their betters are. And this is very well, since it indicates that no historian, however able, is immune from the judgment of his peers in his society, if his preconceptions blur his own judgment.

From the men who write history and are then dragged in fear and trembling before their peers for judgment we have made the traverse to the society of historians which in willing the end of solid footing in the past wills the means by which it is produced, and its quality policed—judgment by peers with all the pain it entails. *But the society of historians is composed of the very people it drags up for judgment. In effect the society of all historians in general wills the torments that each of them undergoes.*

Though many members of the society of professional historians would like to improve the efficiency of its institutions, odd as it may seem, not one, I think, wants to destroy judgment by peers. For however annoying it may be to historians as individuals, still knowing the deep-grained sinfulness of all flesh, they know very well that judgment by peers is what stands between them and slovenliness, pamphleteering, distortion of data, laziness, habitual inaccuracy, dullness beyond the call of duty, and a host of other evils which ultimately and cumulatively would mean the collapse of our society's morale, the frustration of its ends, and therefore, be it noted, the failure of all of us in our calling. Rousseau's conception of the general will as something different not only from the will of each but even from the will of all has sometimes been derided and often is misunderstood. I know of no better illustration of the meaning of the general will than its mode of operation in the society of professional historians in the matter of judgment by peers, where to achieve a recognized and acknowledged common good by a general consent and working through general rules, the will of historians as members of that society imposes itself on the often tough and truculent individual wills of all its members.

The historical relativist and the *aficionado* of the sociology of knowledge profess to be profoundly impressed by the impact of Society on historians. On one side, according to them, there are the sources—the unshaped, unsifted surviving records of the past. And on the other hand is the historian's Society with a big S, which is just about everything that goes on during the historian's lifetime. That Society screeches and roars and hisses in the historian's ear. Each day it passes vividly and living before his eyes. It stinks in his nostrils, and pounds him on the head, and tramples his feet, and squeezes his hands, and tugs at his heart strings, and turns his stomach, and kicks him, and pats him on the back. Of course, with his soul-filling experiences of his Society on one side and the scatter of colorless records of the past on the other, our historian simply impresses on the record whatever is most important or vivid to him at the moment in his current responses to his Society. One thing, however, he appears never to do: he never reads a book by another historian bearing on the historical problem about which he is concerned. In this respect unlike any professional historian for the past century, this Byronic character of the relativists' dream is an absolute unqualified individualist. The fact is that for all their talk about Society, the relativist and the sociologist of knowledge wholly disregard the impact on historians of the only society to which as professionals all historians belong, and thus they miss the true social character of historical work. They disregard the extraordinary extent to which the history that gets written is formed by the society of historians acting through, on, and in the individual historian.

Most of the history written by professionals works within a dual reference system. That system refers him first, to the contemporary sources used by the historian; and second, to the work of other historians used by him—and he is obliged to certify his competence by referring back in his footnotes to the sources and the work of other historians. Under the strong safe cover afforded by this latter obligation the society of historians in arrayed battalions marches square into the work of each of its members. Where there is a "literature" on any subject which an historian deals with he is supposed to know that literature. But to "know the literature" is not to know all the books and articles related somehow or other to the subject. Some books and articles are obsolete, some are trivial and worthless. Some antiquated works will have fallen from the bibliographies and footnotes or because of exemplary incompetence will never even have gotten into them. But the very tasks of genocide and infanticide which lead to this result have been performed for the historian by his society. Nevertheless the number of works by other historians consulted in producing a single monograph often runs into the hundreds, so Carr's precept, "When we take up a work of history our first concern should be not with the facts which it contains but with the historian who wrote it," seems less a counsel of despair than an invitation to madness. In effect, by this point in the history of history writing practically all history is collaborative. The subjects which no historian has touched on before, on which no investigation, even tangential, has been attempted are negligible. Even if he repudiates all current views and regards all previous investigations as tissues of error, an historian must implicitly or explicitly counter those views and undermine those investigations. Even when he does not lean on the work of other historians he must specifically lean away from their work. And such drastic leaning away is the marginal case. The bulk of historical work involves modification rather than subversion.

If, from the beginning, an historian's writing is "socialized" by the necessary employment of the work of other historians, at the end it is "socialized" again through judgment by peers. The apparatus of judgment warns readers of areas of weakness, indicates areas of strength, points to what is obsolete, to what is new and deserving of attention. Finally and most important, the very prospect of judgment by peers socializes the writing of history while the historian is writing it. Knowing that his place in the pecking order, his share of the rewards, and his own estimate of himself, depend on that judgment, he takes pains to do those things his peers approve of and to avoid those that they condemn. What they approve is imaginative compliance with the rules which help to extend the area and increase the firmness of footings for those who seek knowledge of the past. I can only once more express my astonishment that the men who have talked most glibly about the conditioning of the historian by his society have never done at all what is here done rather badly: examine the relation between historians and the society to which they belong, the society on whose estimate of them, their level of income, their

standing among their fellows, and their own judgment
of their life achievement largely depend.

In my penultimate observations I should like to
indulge myself in the luxury of speaking in parables.

Once upon a time three men were considering
going into the import business. Their names were Albert, Bertram, and Claude, or A, B, and C. They were
inlanders who had never seen a freighter, so they came
to a port to have a look around. The first ship Albert
boarded was a miserable old tub. "What's this hulk
for?" Albert asked. He was told it was to carry freight.
Then he went below deck where he saw that the ship
leaked at every seam and that there was three feet of
water in the hold. Albert shrewdly observed, "Sea
water will damage any cargo this wreck carries." And
he was right. The second ship he boarded was in as
bad shape as the first. "Sea water will damage what
this wreck carries, too," he sneered, and he was right
again. Then he visited another ship. He went down
into the hold and he saw an inch of water in it. Being a
clear-headed man, he thought as follows: "All ships
have some water in their holds. Therefore on all ships
the cargo suffers water damage. So it does not matter
what ship you buy cargo from." As a result of this brilliant syllogism he bought indiscriminately. Of course

nobody in the market trusted his judgment, so even when he lucked into a good consignment, he found no customers, so Albert or A went broke. But among people not in the business, he became a sort of hero; and he was called by them an import relativist, because, they said, he had proved that all imports were relatively wet.

Our second man, B or Bertram was a more reflective type than Albert. He, too, inspected several freighters. Taking his clue from the seepage of seawater in all ships, he decided that freighters were apparatus for the collection of oceanographic information. A careful study of seepage would provide data on the nature of the waters which the ship was currently traveling, a sort of sociology of the sea, so to speak. This conclusion had drawbacks, however. On the view that the value of freighters lies in the contribution their bilge water makes to the sociology of the sea, the leakier the tub the better. If freighters are mainly important for their leakiness, why do the better operators take so many pains to make them as watertight as they can? Moreover, whatever contribution the investigations proposed by Bertram might make to oceanography or the sociology of the sea, it is of no use at all to people who want to know which freighters carry clean, dry cargo.

And it was to just this problem of clean cargo that

C or Claude addressed himself. Being a man of drearily systematic habits, he kept lists of freighters and checked their holds on several of their returns to port. He checked with other importers and with under-writers whose interest it was to learn which freighters took good care of their cargo. He knew that even the tightest ships ended their crossings with a little water in the hold; but he also knew exactly how those ships were loaded, so although a bit of their cargo occasion-ally got damaged he rarely bought that part of it. Now he did *not* say that all imports were relatively wet; he said some were wet and some were dry, and that he could tell the difference; so the import relativists called him an absolutist and regarded him as naive. And the fauna and flora in the water that seeped into the bilge did not interest him very much, since what he really was concerned about was the quality of the cargo. So sociologists of the sea thought he was simple-minded and possibly a reactionary. But the other people in the importing line had a different name for him. They called him an old pro.

Here endeth the parable and here almost ends this sociological inquiry. To give a specious penumbra of legitimacy and relevance to my remarks on the import business I will finish with something about a shelf in a library. It is in the British history section. Adjacent to each other on that shelf are Francis Aidan Cardinal

Gasquet's *Henry VIII and the English Monasteries* (1888), and Geoffrey Baskerville's *English Monks and the Suppression of the Monasteries* (1937). Now the historical relativist will smile tolerantly at this juxtaposition because it shows, does it not, what happens when you turn a Catholic and a skeptic loose on the English monasteries and their dissolution? You get just the difference of opinion you would expect, Gasquet all sympathy and Baskerville all sneers, and it is all relative to the social prejudices and prepossessions of the two historians. So it does prove, does it not, that Carr was right after all, and that when "we take up a work of history our first concern should be not with the facts which it contains but with the historian who wrote it."? The sociologist of knowledge, however, observes that the differences are very instructive, since they provide clues to the ideologies current in the 1880s and the 1930s, although of course they tell you nothing for sure about the 1530s. Finally, perhaps an old pro comes by the shelf of the library whereon Gasquet and Baskerville repose. Out of long habit he runs his eyes further down the shelf. There they light on four massive volumes, *The Monastic Order in England* and *The Religious Orders in England.* He observes as he examines that the master of those volumes, the late Regius Professor of Modern History at Cambridge, has taken the infinite pains that the historians are trained to take, in order to keep his cargo free of the seawater of current ideological conflict. Therefore, the old pro does not need long to decide that those volumes rather than Gasquet or Baskerville carry the goods he wants to buy. In fact, all the professional traders have transferred their custom to the late Regius Professor while between occasional and increasingly rare charterings by enthusiastic and incompetent amateurs, Gasquet and Baskerville[7] rot away at the dock. And, of course, it does not matter at all that the late Regius Professor of Modern History at Cambridge, Dom David Knowles, was a Catholic priest and a Benedictine monk. Although, paradoxically, in the context which at the moment concerns us, that it does not matter at all is what matters most of all.

---

7. The above remarks on Geoffrey Baskerville serve to strengthen my skepticism about seat-of-the-pants psychologizing in a way that I would not have chosen to strengthen it. Commenting on an earlier version of the above essay, H. R. Trevor-Roper wrote me, "Allow me to correct you on a point of detail. Geoffrey Baskerville was *not* a skeptic. He was a devout high Anglican. He once told me that he liked to think that no one could deduce his religious views from his historical writing. Which, of course, proves your point." I replied, "Thanks for the point about Geoffrey Baskerville. The error is somewhat embarrassing. On the other hand, it is agreeable to entertain general views so sound that they are confirmed by one's particular mistakes."

Biographical Notes

GOLDWIN SMITH, M.A., Ph.D., D. Litt., F.R.Hist. S., is Professor of History at Wayne State University. He has been a Guggenheim Fellow and a Fellow of the Ford Foundation. Among his published books are *The Treaty of Washington, A History of England, A Constitutional and Legal History of England,* and *The Heritage of Man.* He has contributed articles to journals in the fields of history and philosophy.

A. L. ROWSE, M.A., Ph.D., D.Litt., D.C.L., F.B.A., F.R. Hist. S., Fellow of All Souls College, Oxford, Fellow of the Huntington Library, is one of the foremost historians of our time and an authority on the reign of Elizabeth I. He has published about thirty books of history and poetry, including major biographies of Shakespeare, Sir Richard Grenville, Marlowe, and Sir Walter Raleigh, *The England of Elizabeth, The Elizabethans and America, The Expansion of Elizabethan England, The English Spirit, The Early Churchills,* and *Our Cousin Jacks.*

J. H. HEXTER, M.A., Ph.D., D. Litt., is Charles J. Stillé Professor of History at Yale University. He has been a Guggenheim Fellow, Yaddo Fellow, Fellow of the Ford Foundation, Fellow of the Center for Advanced Study in the Behavioral Sciences, and a Fulbright Fellow. His many books include *The Reign of King Pym; Utopia: The Biography of an Idea; Reappraisals in History; The History Primer.*

This manuscript was prepared for publication by Alice Nigoghosian. The book was designed by Joanne Kinney. The text typeface is Linotype Caledonia designed by W. A. Dwiggins about 1938, and the display face is Caslon's Old Style designed by William Caslon in the eighteenth century.

The text is printed on Perkins & Squier KP Litho paper and the book is bound in Columbia Mills' Fictionette Natural Finish cloth over binders boards. Manufactured in the United States of America.